COUNSELING FOR CHURCH LEADERS

A Practical Guide

BILL BAGENTS

ROSEMARY SNODGRASS

Counseling for Church Leaders

Copyright © 2021 by Bill Bagents and Rosemary Snodgrass

Published by Heritage Christian University Press

Manufactured in the United States of America

Cataloging-in-Publication Data

Bagents, Bill (William Ronald), 1956–

Counseling for church leaders: a practical guide / Bill Bagents and Rosemary Snodgrass

Heritage Christian Leadership Institute Series

p. cm.

ISBN 978-1-7374751-2-5 (paper) 978-1-7374751-3-2 (ebook)

Library of Congress Control Number: 2021913705

1. Pastoral counseling. 2. Counseling. I. Author. II. Snodgrass, Rosemary Black. III. Title. IV. Series.

253.2—dc20

Scripture quotations are from the ESV® Bible (The Holy Bible, English Standard Version®), copyright © 2001 by Crossway, a publishing ministry of Good News Publishers. Used by permission. All rights reserved.

Cover design by Brad McKinnon and Brittany Vander Maas.

All rights reserved. No part of this book may be reproduced in any form or by any electronic or mechanical means, including information storage and retrieval systems, without written permission from the author, except for the use of brief quotations in a book review.

Joint dedication
To the teachers, counselors, and church leaders who have blessed and continue to bless hurting people, may God stand with you as you stand with Him.

Bill's dedication
From Paul Cates to Betty Hamblen to Rosemary Snodgrass, I've been blessed to work with and learn from caring and courageous souls who put their deep hearts on the line to bless others. May God bless you for your effort and your love for struggling souls.

Rosemary's dedication
To Don and our sweet family, leaders one and all.

FOREWORD

MICHAEL D. JACKSON, ED.D.

How often have church leaders been in difficult situations that involve a combination of human emotions and spiritual need? Surveying the frequency of these situations might overwhelmed us. Church leaders are to be commended for being willing to stand in that gap—for rising to the occasion. Far too often, however, it is an occasion for which we are ill-prepared.

That is the genesis of this book. The Heritage Christian Leadership Institute (HCLI) was blessed to have these gifted authors (with countless hours of experience counseling church members and church leaders) agree to help fill the need for a resource that can benefit every kind of church leader. It was an ambitious task! Those who know Bill and Rosemary know that the guidance within this book will be helpful, practical, and insightful. Those who have not yet met them will soon learn just how indispensable this book is for leadership.

My journey of leadership in the church and the world of higher education has taken me through countless hours of elders' meetings, ministry planning meetings, college classes, business meetings, one-on-one conversations, and board meetings. I still remember all of the most difficult conversations and discussions that I've experienced with vivid detail. I can hear myself saying things I shouldn't have said; I can see myself talking instead of listening; I can feel the shock of news I never thought I would hear—and wondering how I would get through it. This book would have helped me in every one of those situations. Perhaps that is my greatest testimony about the value I see in the words you have in your hands.

One of the greatest appreciations that I have for this entry into the leader's toolbox is its unapologetic appeal to Scripture. You will be saturated with counseling guidance for sure, but not absent is the spiritual dimension of that guidance. Entire Bible studies could be created from following the biblical references in several of these chapters—how wonderful it is to have advice grounded in God's truth, and in abundance!

The foundational chapters of this volume are essential to the everyday task of understanding ourselves as leader-counselors, even if we aren't really comfortable with that role! Don't skip the Introduction, where several elements of both motivation and explanation provide you with sure footing for each following chapter. The first nine chapters provide a bedrock upon which the later chapters build. I love the first chapter. What better way to establish a theology of counseling than to appeal to the *theos* Himself?

As a church leader, you will most likely laugh in several places, and for good reason. The situations we find ourselves in sometimes call for humor as the best (or only) medicine. We need to be reminded not to take ourselves too seriously. However, you may also find yourself in tears in sections, feeling the scars of a difficult situation or grief that you have from events all too personal and real. Reading these chapters to help others may, in some sense, be a personal help to you. As leaders we need all the help and support that we can get. (Please don't skip chapter 21!)

My anticipation is that this book will find its way into the Kindles and personal libraries of countless church leaders of all backgrounds and areas of service. It is the kind of entry that can help everyone in some way. I expect it to be read by elders before those meetings that no one wants to have. I suspect that several ministers will pull it off the shelf when a congregant texts with the dreaded words, "We need to talk." I am sure that Bible class teachers will use it both for teaching practice as well as for class content. I know many deacons who need the chapter on helping the angry! Whatever your need, I think you will find great counsel and wisdom in this Godsend of a book.

ACKNOWLEDGEMENTS

Impetus for this book flowed from a request by the leaders of the Heritage Christian Leadership Institute, an arm of Heritage Christian University. We thank President W. Kirk Brothers and Vice President Michael Jackson for their desire to see this done. Dr. Jackson also caught several errors and offered better options as he read an early draft of the book.

The staff of Heritage Christian University Press continues to bless beyond expectations. Executive Director Jamie Cox and Managing Editor Brad McKinnon practice dedication to quality and impressive patience with flawed authors. We thank Brittany Vander Maas for her assistance with the cover.

Laura Lynn Bagents read the developing manuscript multiple times and effected MAJOR improvement. We are grateful.

HERITAGE CHRISTIAN
LEADERSHIP INSTITUTE

"*The Mission of the Heritage Christian Leadership Institute is to provide workshops, seminars, and resources that train godly servant-leaders who can serve as leaders in congregations, families, and communities with an emphasis on training elders and deacons.*"

A Heritage Christian Leadership Institute resource in cooperation with Heritage Christian University Press

BIBLE ABBREVIATIONS

Old Testament
    Gen   Genesis
    Exod   Exodus
    Lev   Leviticus
    Num   Numbers
    Deut   Deuteronomy
    Josh   Joshua
    Judg   Judges
    Ruth   Ruth
    1–2 Sam   1–2 Samuel
    1–2 Kgs   1–2 Kings
    1–2 Chr   1–2 Chronicles
    Ezra   Ezra
    Neh   Nehemiah
    Esth   Esther
    Job   Job
    Ps   Psalms
    Prov   Proverbs
    Eccl   Ecclesiastes

Song	Song of Solomon
Isa	Isaiah
Jer	Jeremiah
Lam	Lamentations
Ezek	Ezekiel
Dan	Daniel
Hos	Hosea
Joel	Joel
Amos	Amos
Obad	Obadiah
Jonah	Jonah
Mic	Micah
Nah	Nahum
Hab	Habakkuk
Zeph	Zephaniah
Hag	Haggai
Zech	Zechariah
Mal	Malachi

New Testament

Matt	Matthew
Mark	Mark
Luke	Luke
John	John
Acts	Acts
Rom	Romans
1–2 Cor	1–2 Corinthians
Gal	Galatians
Eph	Ephesians
Phil	Philippians
Col	Colossians
1–2 Thess	1–2 Thessalonians

1–2 Tim	1–2 Timothy
Titus	Titus
Phlm	Philemon
Heb	Hebrews
Jas	James
1–2 Pet	1–2 Peter
1–2–3 John	1–2–3 John
Jude	Jude
Rev	Revelation

CONTENTS

Introduction	1
1. God as Counselor	12
2. Wellness	23
3. What Should & Shouldn't Scare People About Counseling	35
4. Why Do People Seek Counseling?	50
5. The Basics of Listening	61
6. The Basics of Empathy	73
7. The Basics of Emotion	85
8. Traps to Avoid	99
9. Recognizing Mental Illness and Making Effective Referrals	112
10. Helping the Angry	125
11. Helping the Depressed	137
12. Helping the Fearful	147
13. Helping the Grieving	159
14. Helping the Under-Connected	171
15. Helping People Unstick	183
16. Helping People Upgrade Their Habits	194
17. When We Must Share Bad News	207
18. Dealing with Toxic People	218
19. Self-Esteem and Selfishness	231
20. The Power of Prevention	244
21. Taking Sufficient Care of Ourselves	256
Recommended Resources	267
Works Cited	271
Scripture Index	276

About the Authors	277
Also by Heritage Christian University Press in Cooperation with Heritage Christian Leadership Institute	279

COUNSELING FOR CHURCH LEADERS

INTRODUCTION

In Defense of Our Title

By definition, Christians help people. Helping others is central to following Jesus. "The Son of Man did not come to be served, but to serve" (Matt 20:28). While salvation was the ultimate mission of Jesus, He improved people's lives in countless ways. His promise of abundant life leads to eternity with God, but it lacks neither value nor meaning while we're still on earth (John 10:10, Acts 2:44–47, Rom 12:9–21, Eph 4:17–32).

In our era, "counseling" is the major descriptor for the kind of people-helping advocated in this book. You need not love the word "counseling" to benefit from this book. We'd never argue that you should endorse everything that's done in the name of counseling—that covers bizarre, diverse, and ever-changing territory. Our initial request is modest: Please let us use "counseling" as shorthand for seeking to help others through a combination of caring, exploring, listening, teaching, and understanding.

We aren't speaking of counseling in a clinical sense as practiced by mental health professionals. We aren't even speaking of church leaders with special training. We're speaking of loving hearts, willing to care and trying to be of service in the name of Jesus. We're speaking from Scripture. "Rejoice with those who rejoice, weep with those who weep" (Rom 12:15). "Let each of you look not only to his own interests, but also to the interests of others" (Phil 2:4). "If God so loved us, we also ought to love one another" (1 John 4:11). "Bear one another's burdens, and so fulfill the law of Christ" (Gal 6:2). We're supporting the faithful leadership and ministry described in 2 Timothy 2:1–7 and Titus 2:1–8. We're speaking of being real with people as we help one another live in the light of God's word.

Christians have a healthy tendency toward humility. What does that look like in our context? "Don't call me a counselor. Don't call what I did counseling. All I did was listen." Did you listen with love? Did the Lord use your listening to bless others? If the person to whom you listened gave glory to God, you did well. If the person felt encouraged, enlightened, or even just slightly better, you did well. We won't complain if you call your work something other than counseling.

From another perspective, we're thinking of counseling as "grandma stuff," the kind of safe, wise, honest, loving, and practical guidance that a dear Christian "grammie" shares with her beloved descendants. But don't let "guidance" mislead you. It's about far more than the giving of advice. Ecclesiastes 3:7 reminds us that there's "a time to keep silence, and a time to speak." Proverbs 29:11 more bluntly says, "A fool gives full vent to his spirit, but a wise man quietly holds it back." Healthy people don't say everything that they think. Good grandmas and good counselors know the value of long listening, slow speaking, and letting God have time to work (Jas 1:19–20). This book isn't a set of formulas, guarantees, and easy answers.

Counseling for Church Leaders is a loaded phrase. It demands both a definition of counseling and of church leaders. While we don't mind preachers reading this book, it's not a book for preachers. We're thinking of church leaders in the broadest sense.

Biblically, we're coming from Galatians 6:1: "Brethren, if anyone is caught in any trespass, you who are spiritual should restore him in a spirit of gentleness." Scripture doesn't limit "you who are spiritual" to those who hold a special role or title. Like Paul, we're thinking of any Christian blessed with sufficient love, wisdom, and spirituality to offer help to others in the name of Jesus.

Biblically, we're coming from Titus 2:1 and 1 Timothy 4:11–5:2, where even young evangelists have something to offer those who are older in years. We're coming from Titus 2:3–5, where older women have much to offer younger ladies. We're remembering Ephesians 4:11–16, where the body grows in maturity and stability "when each part is working properly." And we're remembering that not every part of the body has the same skills and gifts (1 Cor 12, Rom 12:4–13).

When we think of church leaders, we're thinking of both formal and informal roles, both public and private service, both young and old, and both men and women in any sphere where God approves our service.

THE INEVITABILITY OF COUNSELING FOR CHURCH LEADERS

If you care about and interact with people, you will find yourself in a counseling role. The frequency and depth of that role will vary depending on your personality, the number of people you know, and countless other factors. Without doubt, you will be someone's choice of listening ear and caring heart. This scares the daylights out of many church leaders.

Leaders respond differently to distrust of counseling, fear of counseling, lack of expertise, or lack of desire to counsel. (No, that list is not exhaustive nor are these four categories mutually exclusive.) As implied above, some deny a leadership role: "I have no title, no business card, no formal recognition. I'm not a leader. I didn't sign up for this. It's not my responsibility." Galatians 6:1-2 and Philippians 2:3-4 beg to differ. Ultimately, some may be as honest as Moses in Exodus 4:10-13. To paraphrase, "Lord, I'm out of excuses. I don't want to do this. Pick someone else; pick anybody else." God didn't honor Moses's request.

Some congregations delegate all counseling needs to their preacher or to some other person deemed as "most qualified." Counseling as defined in this book can't be delegated away. When people seek our help, they have extended a measure of trust and opportunity. By their choice, they've paid us a compliment. There's a reason they chose us. Not helping is not a loving option. If only "the most qualified individual" fills every role of service, overload and burnout are certain. None of us become qualified by doing nothing. We all learn on the job.

Bluntly, counseling is too important to leave to counselors. The needs are far too vast. There are not enough professionals for every need to be addressed on a professional level. Not everyone can afford professional help. Not every professional understands spiritual concerns. Not every issue needs professional help. With all due respect to the wisdom of making a referral to a professional when that is best, most needs don't rise to that level. Many of our friends already know what to do; they just need validation, motivation, and support. They need to know they're not alone. Even for those who need professional help, many will need our support in finding the strength to take that next step.

Don't underestimate the power of trying. When people ask us for help and we make an effort, that effort becomes a powerful statement of love. It says, "You matter. You're not alone. I care. God cares. Don't give up." God can make much of our little.

A WORD ABOUT SCRIPTURE

We believe and value the Bible as God's word. We take 2 Timothy 3:10–17 to heart. We believe Scripture is from God, understandable, faith-producing, and action-guiding. We believe Scripture is indeed "able to make you wise for salvation through faith in Christ Jesus." We believe Scripture is profitable and equipping. We intend to live, teach, and counsel under the authority of Scripture.

Many sentences throughout this book end with biblical citations. Please read them. Are we being fair with Scripture in context? If so, what does that mean for your confidence and understanding? If not, we welcome you to give us the opportunity to learn "the way of God more accurately" (Acts 18:26). We don't see ourselves as experts without flaws. (Would you believe the first time I typed that, it came out "experts without falw"?)

A BRIEF HISTORY OF THE CARE OF SOULS

Logically, the human side of the care of souls (people helping, counseling in its earliest unnamed form) had to begin with family. Who else was there? Perhaps, there were rare individuals who were gifted with extra insight and understanding. Predominately, we think of small family groups who valued the wisdom and experience of their older members. Abraham and Job exemplify this group (Gen 18:19, Job 1:1–5).

We see a major example of family counseling family in Ruth 2:17ff. Naomi's questions about Ruth's successful gleaning stirred embers of hope. God had not forsaken; God was obviously at work. As Ruth 3 begins, Naomi was coaching the young Moabitess in the bizarre (from our perspective) details of how to express her appreciation to and interest in Boaz. Love, trust, interest, effort, education, and conversation led to a blessed outcome.

Exodus 18:13–27 offers another example. Jethro, Moses's father-in-law, saw Moses practicing an unsustainable leadership model. He was trying to judge every case on every level for the entire nation. "What you are doing is not good!" is classic understatement (Exod 18:17). To his credit, Moses listened, took the matter to the Lord, and made the approved changes.

To be fair, stunning negative examples can be cited,

none more tragic than Jonadab's advice to Amnon in 2 Samuel 13:1–6. Listening to his cousin cost Amnon both his life and his reputation. Sadly, Solomon's wives "turned away his heart after other gods" (1 Kgs 11:1–5). Ahab was terrible on his own, but he was worse with Jezebel's counsel (1 Kgs 21:1–16).

We think next of trusted religious leaders. Moses and Joshua stand as clear biblical examples (Exod 34:29–35, Josh 1:1–9). We think of Stephanas (1 Cor 16:15–16) and elders in the church (Heb 13:7, 17; 1 Tim 3:1–7). Your authors work in conservative religious environments where notable respect remains for both family and religious leaders whose lives are recognized as congruent with Scripture.

Again, in a spirit of fairness, religious leaders aren't always right. There's the famous warning of Deuteronomy 13:1–5. Even a prophet or dreamer who could produce both a sign and a wonder was not to be followed if he tried to lead God's people to other gods. It was never a matter of "blindly follow your religious leaders no matter what." From Aaron (Exod 32) to the false prophets who opposed Jeremiah (Jer 23) to those who taught falsely about Jesus (2 John 7–8), examples of bad counsel from religious leaders abound.

After the Enlightenment, trust in religious authority waned. The flaws of many patriarchs and church leaders are well-documented. Trust turned more toward the sciences of anthropology, psychology, and sociology. Freud introduced the world to the id, ego, superego, the unconscious, and defense mechanisms. People helping moved from the purview of religion to the realm of the social sciences. Truth became truer when spoken or penned by an expert with a PhD. Please know that we both have benefitted from higher education and mean no disrespect to learning. At the same time, a terminal degree is no guarantee of either wisdom or veracity.

It's also wise to remember that the social sciences don't present a unified theory of human nature, function, or wellness. There are competing theories of personality, motivation, and therapeutic interventions. It would be absurd to think of the social sciences as monolithic.

In our postmodern age, we have a confusing mixture of trust in experts and mistrust of everything. For some, individuals are deemed to create their own truth and reality. Perhaps you have friends who know the latest mental health or life skills recommendation must be true "because I Googled it and it sounds so good." Others assume accuracy of information because "it feels so right" or "I just know."

Of course, this thinnest of sketches should not imply neat, linear categories. Some still listen to family members above all others. Some notably trust their religious leaders. Others consistently seek the judgment of recognized authorities who are informed by the latest research. The chief value of this section lies in the reminder that there are competing voices regarding values, behavior, and reality. As we contemplate the possibility of helping others, we're reminded that people have radically different understandings of what it means to be human, what it means to be healthy or well, what it means to be moral, and even the purpose of life.

ANOTHER ASPECT OF THE CARE OF SOULS

The relationship between mental health needs and other life needs (for example, help with relationships, communication, personal development, and spirituality) is complex. Some might choose to remove themselves from any service related to counseling due to their errant belief that, since counseling deals with mental health issues, it must be left to highly trained experts.

Mental health issues exist. A person battling a psychosis needs clinical and medical assistance at a professional level. To think ourselves qualified to treat that person would be stunningly sad. Fortunately, the vast majority of mental health issues are not on that level. For a person battling non-clinical depression or excessive worry, the support of a trusted friend can have major benefits.

More importantly, most people who seek help from church leaders are not seeking assistance with mental health issues. As we'll discuss in chapter three, their needs, while real and important, flow much more frequently from the stress and complexity of daily life. *How do I worry less and find more peace? Why am I not happier? How do I deal with my anger? How can I listen better? How can I communicate more effectively? Why aren't my kids more respectful? Why am I not closer to my spouse? How do I find my purpose in life, my niche, my reason for existence? Is God pleased with me? How do I learn to forgive? I believe I'm walking with Jesus, so why don't I feel forgiven? Am I normal? Why don't I feel normal? Am I a hypocrite if I act better than I feel, or if I do what's right even when I don't really want to?*

Those are real-world questions—and they're just the hem of the garment. Those are not questions that require professional intervention. They're questions that God addresses through Scripture and through the wisdom of those who walk with Him. They're questions to which church leaders can speak. And it's always an honor to speak a good word for the Lord. If church leaders don't address them, the world will. And, even at its best, the world will leave Jesus out of the discussion.

WHY READ THIS BOOK?

As Christians, we're in the people-helping business. Our biggest concern is their souls, but we care on every level. We want people to be whole and healthy. We want families to be stable and strong. We want churches to be close and caring. We want communities to be peaceful and productive. As church leaders, we're going to counsel others in an effort to help them.

As Christians, we want to give our best to God. We know the first and second commandments of Matthew 22:34–40. We appreciate the biblical concept of giving our best to God. We honor and embrace Colossians 3:23: "Whatever you do, work heartily as to the Lord and not for men." We love the "more and more" principle of 1 Thessalonians 4:9–10. Our goal is to be "always abounding in the work of the Lord" (1 Cor 15:58).

So why wrestle with this book? You already know: to add tools to our toolbox, to maximize our effectiveness in God's service, and so our best can get better. That's the positive side of the equation, but the other side is just as important. Wrestle with this book so you'll make fewer mistakes, have fewer regrets, and sleep better at night.

It's not Scripture, but it's true: The First Rule of Counseling is "Do no harm," aka "Don't make it worse." Even with maximum love and prayer, we won't get it right every time we try to help others. Even with the best of intentions, we will err. Even if we make no error at all, people will sometimes reject our help (Gen 4:6–8, Matt 23:37–39). At the end of the day, we want to be able to pass the mirror test. We want to be able to look in the mirror of God's word and say, "I tried. I did my best."

"Don't make it worse" merits a word of caution. Even when we do our best to help others, they sometimes feel worse before progress is evident. There's often a delay between doing better and feeling better. Regrettably, on other occasions things get worse despite our best effort. Again, think of God's conversation with Cain in Genesis 4. Cain's actions and consequences took a terrible turn, but NOT because God tried to help him. The devil loves for us to misjudge our motives, over-process negative outcomes, and assign ourselves unwarranted blame so we'll stop trying to do the difficult work of helping others.

We can offer no guarantees. We happily acknowledge that we don't know what we don't know. It would be the height of arrogance for us to assert that this book is THE book. But we believe every Scripture cited herein. We invite you to think with us and to add what you know to the mix.

CHAPTER 1
GOD AS COUNSELOR

One of the greatest examples of God's greatness is His humility in the midst of eternal perfection. The Almighty, who needs nothing and owes no one anything, chooses to interact with people—His rebellious and flawed creatures. We will examine some of God's interactions with people where His obvious intention was to help them. That's what we mean by God as Counselor: God willingly and lovingly in the role of people helper, God both leading and serving by offering His help to those in both need and danger.

As we note these examples of God's actions, we'll address key questions. What is God modeling for us? What should we be learning from Him? Why is God doing what He's doing? How were His efforts received? What should we learn from how His efforts were received?

GOD WITH ADAM AND EVE

Post sin, their eyes are opened, and the first people attempt to hide from God. It would be funny if it weren't so sad—trying to hide from the all-knowing omnipresent One. It isn't a case of the sinners seeking God for forgiveness. Rather, Genesis 3:9ff tells us that God comes seeking Adam and Eve. We know this because God asks, "Where are you?" (Gen 3:15)

"Where are you?" is the first of at least four questions that God poses for Adam and Eve. Often, we ask questions because we need information. It's never so with God. God, who is all-knowing, knows exactly where they are, exactly what they have done, the reasoning they've employed (or failed to employ), and the motives from which they are acting. Why does God pose a series of questions? He asks to start a conversation, to give Adam and Eve opportunity to reflect, and to show them that He still loves them.

In His first people-helping conversation, God models the power of effective questions. Adam and Eve's responses leave much to be desired. Adam blames both Eve and God. Eve attempts to shift blame to the serpent and offers the excuse that she has been deceived. Still, we love the fact that God initiates the conversation and gives them opportunity for truth, confession, and request for His help.

GOD WITH CAIN

Pre-murder, God sees the peril awaiting Cain. His feelings have been hurt, his sacrifice has been rejected, and he has looked bad before his family. Cain is angry. His face shows his pain (Gen 4:5). God knows that Cain's very soul is in danger.

Knowing the goodness of God, we're not surprised that He chooses to intervene. First the Lord questions Cain's overall reaction, particularly his anger. "Why are you angry, and why has your face fallen?" (Gen 4:8) How should we hear those questions? Possibilities abound: "You would be wise to explore the nature of your anger. Are you angry with the right person—yourself?" "Are you angry in the right manner—angry that you have disappointed God?" "Are you angry in the right degree—angry enough to be motivated to repent, but not angry enough to compound your sin?"

Those who have tried to help angry people see the brilliance of God's questions. Anger often shuts down higher-order thinking. Inviting angry people to think invites them to step back from their anger. If people will think, they can gain perspective. If people will think, they can foresee and weigh likely consequences of their potential actions.

Notice how God offers Cain hope and encouragement. "If you do well, will you not be accepted?" (Gen 4:6) God is saying, "This is nowhere near hopeless. You have not destroyed your life. No door has been permanently closed. Your destiny is still within your control. You still have choices, good choices. You can still do right and reap the rewards."

When people err in public, they often feel an extra sting. *Everybody saw. Everybody knows. I've been judged. I'll always be judged. Life is broken beyond repair. It doesn't matter what I do next. I'm ruined.* In such situations, there's tremendous power in offering hope. The Bible utterly rejects fatalism.

The offer must be both legitimate and realistic, but God makes that so much easier for us. Looking forward in Scripture, we see a murdering adulterer forgiven and allowed to serve as king. We see a denier preaching on Pentecost. We see a persecutor appointed as apostle to the Gentiles. One of our greatest roles in helping people is extending hope and reminding people of God's power to forgive.

Not only does God extend an offer of help, pose great questions, and offer hope, He also offers Cain a spiritual perspective on his situation. In this regard, church leaders who try to help others stand firmly with God. "If you do not do well, sin is crouching at the door" (Gen 4:7). We can't read that line from the ESV without remembering 1 Peter 5:8, "Be sober-minded, be watchful. Your adversary the devil prowls around like a roaring lion, seeking someone to devour." Crouching or prowling, this evil lion plans to eat.

Again, there's no fatalism. God says of sin, "Its desire is for you, but you must rule over it" (Gen 4:7). What a statement! "You must rule over it" necessarily implies that you can rule over it. With God's help, you have the strength, wisdom, and insight. Don't cave. Step up. Make the Godward choice. What a message of hope and faith!

How were God's efforts repaid? You know how the story ends. "Cain rose up against his brother Abel and killed him" (Gen 4:8). Cain rejected God's counsel, committed murder, and then tried to cover his sin. God did not fail Cain; Cain failed both God and himself. Cain received perfect counsel and rejected it. He did the very opposite of what God taught him.

These facts hold tremendous power for every Christian who tries to help others. God rightly holds us responsible for our attitudes, words, and actions. The Lord does not hold us responsible for people's responses to our godly efforts. This is clearly taught in the famous watchman passage, Ezekiel 33. It's just as clearly exemplified in Jesus's encounter with the rich young ruler. The young man did not leave in sorrow because Jesus failed him. He left in pain because he failed to live up to what he knew to be true (Mark 10:17–22). When it comes to helping people, what counts is faithful, loving effort rather than the ultimate result. If we cannot accept this truth, we won't last long as people helpers. If we try to bear the responsibility of others, we will crumble under the irrational load.

GOD WITH JOB

Job's is an astonishingly difficult story. Why would the Lord point out Job to His evil adversary (Job 1:8)? Why would God allow Satan to take so much from Job? Why would God allow Job's friends (frenemies?) to be so stunningly wrong in their assessment of Job's situation? What right do I have as a creature, finite and flawed, to question the Almighty?

Sometimes God doesn't tell us all that we want to know. In Job's case, He doesn't offer even a hint of an answer. On the plus side are two key statements: Even facing cataclysmic loss, "In all this Job did not sin or charge God with wrong" (Job 1:22). And in one of Scripture's fiercest statements of faith, "Though He slay me, I will hope in Him." (Job 13:15).

On the other side of the coin, even Job makes major assumptions that do not serve him well. Half of Job 13:15 is quoted above. The other half states, "yet I will argue my ways to His face." Job believes that God owes him an answer. Job believes that he would be blessed in some way if God would just explain Himself. To his credit, Job pivots to humble repentance when God falsifies his assumptions (Job 38:1–42:6, especially 40:3–5 and 42:1–6).

What does Job teach us about efforts to help people? Far more happens in the unseen realms than we know or understand (Job 1–2, Eph 6:12). Sometimes our lifelong friends can be miserable counselors, making horrible assumptions (Job 4:7). Sometimes we can deceive ourselves by thinking, "If I only knew why this was happening, I could bear it better." Any of us can fall into the trap of imagining that God owes us answers. There may be answers that we're incapable of processing even if they were clearly stated. Knowing the reasons behind a great loss does nothing to quell the pain of that loss.

What implications for counseling can church leaders draw from the story of Job? Watch our assumptions. Practice humility. Only God always knows the whole story. Don't speak where God is silent. Don't say more than we know to be true. Let God be God. Don't go beyond the word.

Sometimes, silence is the very best course of action (Job 2:11–13). There are problems we can't solve. There are problems that defy solution. There are questions that can't be answered. There are needs we can't meet, no matter how much we try or how deeply we love. To quote the great philosopher Clint Eastwood, "A man's got to know his limitations."

In the end, God blesses the faithful. God always does right. God is always trustworthy. God is always God. We trust God based on His self-revelation. Sometimes, we find ourselves trusting God because there's no other sensible choice. Though He loves us and constantly draws near, there is no gulf in the universe as great as the gulf between creature and Creator. We are incapable of understanding how great He is and how limited we are.

Job's bottom line for us: Don't try to explain the inexplicable. Don't say more than God reveals. Never blame the victim. Revere God, even in the darkest of times.

GOD WITH DAVID

After David's greatest set of sins, God sent the prophet Nathan to his lost and damaged king. While Nathan mouths the words, he speaks God's truth in 2 Samuel 12. The key element of this encounter is truth telling through narrative, using story and metaphor to speak to the heart.

We feel sorry for Nathan on this mission. He could be killed for confronting his king. To his credit, God sends and he goes. It's an outstanding example of courage. Is it also a reminder that we need not desire or delight in the mission God gives us. People helping isn't always easy or pleasant. As servants of God and doers of good, our job is to hear God and obey.

We know the famous story of the horrible rich man and the poor man's pet lamb. We understand why this story is perfect for David. He has risked his life to protect sheep that, to the best of our knowledge, were never "like a daughter to him" (1 Sam 17:33–37). Think of all the psalms where David speaks of shepherd and sheep (Ps 78:70–72, Ps 79:13, Ps 95:6–7, Ps 100:3), none more famous than Psalm 23.

What are the implications for church leaders who counsel? Clearly, we recognize the power of metaphor and story. We recognize the power of speaking to both the head and the heart. We remember that the most direct approach isn't always the best approach. We see that helping sinful people confront themselves is far superior when our goal is repentance and restoration.

Even when we are blessed to bring people to the cusp of life-changing insight, we must summon the courage to take the next step, to clearly say what God would have us say. Nathan excels in courage and clarity (2 Sam 12:7–12). We don't think of him as gloating, but he doesn't mince words. We don't see him as reveling in the moment when he gives a king his comeuppance. We see him as God's instrument doing all that he can to "save a soul from death and cover a multitude of sins" (Jas 5:19–20). We see him doing God's merciful work, snatching a soul out of the fire (Jude 22–23).

GOD WITH ELIJAH

We will reserve 1 Kings 19, one of Scripture's classic people helping encounters, for chapter 11 "Helping the Depressed." Please note that it powerfully fits this chapter as well.

GOD WITH HIS CHOSEN PEOPLE

We include a discussion of Isaiah 1 because it, like Nathan's confrontation of David, presents the teaching aspect of offering God's corrective counsel. It does not employ a heartrending story. Rather, it features clear, direct presentation of facts with both powerful metaphors and strong emphasis on the consequences of sinful actions. It's logical and cognitive to the core. There's no beating around the bush, no mincing of words. Both lives and souls are at stake.

God's people have rebelled (Isa 1:2). Even the ox and the donkey don't forget their masters, but God's people have forgotten (Isa 1:3). God's people have broken faith with Him (Isa 1:4). And they are reaping terrible consequences (Isa 1:5–9). They still observe religious rituals, but those acts hold no meaning for God (Isa 1:10–15). As bad as things are, the situation isn't hopeless. Repentance and restoration are possible (Isa 1:16–17). Think. Consider your ways. You're on the path to death and destruction. Choose life with God (Isa 1:18–20).

Are there occasions when church leaders must be this blunt when offering help to others? Yes. We suggest the following implications from Isaiah 1. While not fans of Dr. Phil's practice of televising the struggles of vulnerable people, we appreciate the wisdom of his trademark question: "How's that working out for you?" That's the question God asks through Isaiah. "Can't you see what's happening to you?" "Do you call your present state of affairs desirable?" "Do you want to continue down this path?" "Can't you see that it ends in death?"

These questions aren't threats. They're stout calls to

realistic assessment. "Please stop pretending." "End the denial." "There's no path forward until we get real."

Note that God clearly presents a reality check, but He tempers its stoutness with hope. He reminds His people that they can choose their behavior, that they have superior options (Isa 1:5). Things don't have to continue as they are. He reminds them that He can neither accept their worship nor hear their prayers as they continue in rebellion (Isa 1:11–15). He also invites them to wash themselves and make themselves clean, to learn to do good again (Isa 1:16–17).

No matter how far people fall, we don't fall outside the reach of God's grace. As long as there is breath, there is hope. That's one of the highest motivations for helping people in the name of God. He can forgive any sin that we will renounce. He can restore any trust that we break. He takes no delight in the death of the wicked (Ezek 33:11). His will has always been to save rather than to destroy (John 3:16–17, 1 Tim 2:3–6).

Yes, this is an unapologetic appeal to church leaders to reach out to the rebellious, to both those who are aggressive/hostile and those who are passive/unaware. We offer four reasons. Doing so reflects what God has done for us; it follows God's example (Rom 5:6–8). Doing so makes us obedient servants of God (2 Cor 5:13–21, 1 Tim 2:3–5). As in Isaiah's day, a faithful remnant will hear and answer. Some will choose to be reconciled to God. Finally, even if most don't welcome our efforts, we'll be better for having tried.

OBJECTIONS TO THE CONCEPT OF GOD AS COUNSELOR

"It's both presumptuous and blasphemous to present God as The First and Greatest Therapist. We intend no such presentation. The focus of this book isn't therapy. Our focus is choosing to help people draw near to God and live better in Christ by showing them the love of God and the wisdom of living God's way. God is love, God loves people, and love acts to bless people.

"Intervening in people's lives, aka meddling in their business, is fine for God. He's the Creator. He's all-knowing. He never errs. We often err. We need to leave people-helping to Him." The most effective deceptions contain maximum statements of truth. God is perfect, infinitely superior to us in every way. Yet, God lives in us and works through us. God commissions us to love and do good works (Gal 6:10, Eph 2:10, Titus 2:7 & 14, 3:8 & 14). We are instructed to "look to the interests of others" (Phil 2:4) and to "bear one another's burdens" (Gal 6:2).

"We'll never be able to perfectly imitate God's love." That's true. We also won't be able to perfectly imitate His holiness, but that's still the standard taught by Scripture (1 Pet 1:13–16). His love remains both our motivation and our standard (1 John 4:9–11). Our love for God merits more than our best effort. It also merits every effort to make our best better. We keep adding skills, wisdom, knowledge, and spiritual maturity so we'll be ever more able to serve God and His people. Even at our best we maintain the perspective and humility of Luke 17:5–10, but we take great heart in the fact that God allows us to serve in His name and to His glory.

CHAPTER 2

WELLNESS

KEEPING OUR GOALS CLEAR

In the introduction, we asserted that those who are spiritual "fulfill the law of Christ" by helping others bear their burdens (Gal 6:1–2). We have also acknowledged that all of us are "wounded healers," both imperfect and unaware of all our imperfections (Rom 3:23). In that "the heart is deceitful above all things, and desperately sick" and "every way of a man is right in his own eyes," how can we know that we're sound enough to help others (Jer 17:9, Prov 21:2)? We respect the warnings of Proverbs 26:12, Romans 12:3, and 1 Corinthians 10:12. The healthier we are as helpers, the stronger our access to God's wisdom and power. Negatively stated, the blinder and weaker we are, the more limited our ability to help. Even worse, the "less well" we are, the greater the likelihood that we'll discourage and mislead others.

In addition to using this chapter for personal assessment and growth as helpers, it can also serve to guide us as we help others. Toward what goals are we helping them? Do those goals flow from God? Biblically speaking, what should we want to help people become? What does wellness (wholeness, soundness) include? What values and practices contribute to the pursuit of wellness?

LESSER GOALS

As Christians, our goal can't be just to help others feel better regardless of their actions and their relationship with God. That version of acceptance is unhealthy and unbiblical. Our goal can't be to tell people only what they want to hear. Most people are already amazingly adept at telling themselves what they want to hear. Our goal can't be merely to minimize conflict, whether interpersonal and intrapersonal. "A life without conflict" is a pipedream. Without some degree of conflict—at least at the level of realizing that I'm not all that I should be, there's no motivation to improve. Certainly, our goal can't be to help others feel superior by comparing themselves with fellow strugglers.

EIGHT ASPECTS OF BIBLICAL WELLNESS

Even if our list is incomplete, we're certain about the primacy of the first item. To be well, we need to see ourselves as God sees us. Admittedly, we can't do this perfectly, but we'll be all the better for trying. James describes this as looking into "the perfect law, the law of liberty" like one looks at his face in a mirror (Jas 1:22–25). Paul gives us the famous encouragement, "Examine yourselves, to see whether you are in the faith. Test yourselves" (2 Cor 13:5). We sense the resonance as we read 1 Corinthians 4:1–5 in light of Matthew 7:1–5.

To speak more emotively, we remember Psalm 139:23–24, "Search me, O God, and know my heart! Try me, and know my thoughts! And see if there be any wicked way in me, and lead me in the way everlasting." That psalm has the most beautiful bookends. It begins with recognition of God's complete knowledge of us—even our thoughts and our yet-to-be-spoken words. And it ends with a plea that God continue to search us, know us, lead us, and shape us. Woven into the psalm is the desire to see ourselves as God sees us so that we can become more like Him.

Luke 18:9–14 and John 5:31–47 offer stunning examples of spiritual blindness. The Pharisee and the religious hierarchy as a whole had no concept of their standing before God. That blindness left them unable to help in God's name or to be helped by God's Son. Isaiah 1 offers another example. Ancient Israel could not see how their worship offended God because of their rebellion and spiritual bankruptcy.

On multiple occasions, Jesus pulls back the curtain to show us God's view of people. The centurion demonstrated more faith than anyone in Israel (Luke 7:9). The sinful woman of Luke 7:36–50 demonstrated exemplary love and saving faith. Zacchaeus was a son of Abraham (Luke 19:9). Jesus said of the widow who gave the two tiny coins, "Truly, I tell you this poor widow has put in more than all of them" (Luke 21:3). Each of these encounters demonstrates the truth of 1 Samuel 16:7: "For the Lord sees not as man sees; man looks on the outward appearance, but the Lord looks on the heart."

The second aspect of wellness is living congruently with our beliefs, given that our beliefs flow from and are governed by Scripture.

> And now, Israel, what does the Lord your God require of you, but to fear the Lord your God, to walk in all His ways, to love Him, to serve the Lord your God with all your heart and with all your soul, and to keep the commandments and statutes of the Lord, which I am commanding you today for your good? (Deut 10:12–13)

We acknowledge that we need God's guidance (Prov 16:25, 21:2; Jer 10:23–24). Consistency between belief and conduct is emphasized in Scripture from both positive and negative perspectives. "Not everyone who says to Me, 'Lord, Lord,' will enter the kingdom of heaven, but the one who does the will of My Father in heaven" (Matt 7:21). "The scribes and the Pharisees sit on Moses' seat, so practice and observe whatever they tell you—but not what they do. For they preach and do not practice" (Matt 23:2–3). "They profess to know God, but they deny Him by their works" (Titus 1:16). "If we say we have fellowship with Him while we walk in darkness, we lie and do not practice the truth" (1 John 1:6).

"Even a child makes himself known by his acts, by whether his conduct is pure and upright" (Prov 20:11). "And He who sent Me is with Me. He has not left Me alone, for I always do those things that please Him" (John 8:29). "In the first book, O Theophilus, I have dealt with all the things that Jesus began to do and teach" (Acts 1:1). Good conduct and fidelity enable believers to "adorn the doctrine of God our Savior" (Titus 2:10). "Little children, let us not love in word or talk but in deed and in truth" (1 John 3:17).

The third aspect of biblical wellness is having a proper orientation toward others, recognizing the fundamental worth and brotherhood of humanity as God's creation. Genesis 1:26–27 powerfully describes all of humanity as made in the image of God. Acts 17:22–29 records Paul's sermon, which includes these encouraging statements: "And He made from one man every nation of mankind to live on all the face of the earth," and "For we are all indeed His offspring."

The Bible's most well-known verse speaks of God's love for every person (John 3:16). Is there a more compelling parable than The Good Samaritan (Luke 10)? Could Jesus have more clearly taught the brotherhood of humanity? The Great Commission emphasizes the importance of every soul to God (Matt 28:18–20). Paul emphasizes humanity's universal obligation to care for one another in Galatians 6:10: "So, then, as we have opportunity, let us do good to everyone."

The fourth component of spiritual wellness is having a proper sense of self. We base our self-worth in the fact that we are all created in the image of God (Gen 1:26–27). We remember how Scripture describes us, "Yet You have made him a little lower than the heavenly beings and have crowned him with glory and honor. You have given him dominion over the works of Your hands." (Ps 8:5–6). The value of a proper sense of self-worth is supported by Philippians 2:3–4, where we are instructed to look not only to our own interests, "but also to the interests of others." Ephesians 5:28 appeals brilliantly to the godly view of self-worth: "In the same way husbands should love their wives as their own bodies."

Most of us know the JOY acronym: Jesus, Others, Yourself. It reminds us that the biblical teaching on self-worth is NOT selfishness; it is not "self first." Jesus opposes "self first" in Luke 9:23–24: "If anyone would come after Me, let him deny himself, and take up his cross daily and follow Me. For whoever would save his life will lose it, but whoever loses his life for My sake will save it." Paul reminds us that love, as defined by God, "does not insist on its own way" (1 Cor 13:5). Galatians 5:20 lists jealousy and rivalries, obvious manifestations of selfishness, among the works of the flesh. The list of terrible behaviors that describe the last days begins, "for people will be lovers of self" (2 Tim 3:1–5). Only with God's help will we find the biblical balance that we need to be well and whole.

A fifth aspect of wellness is having a sense of personal responsibility that allows others to shoulder their personal responsibility. God documented that sense of personal responsibility when He held Adam, Eve, and Cain accountable for their actions (Gen 3–4). The balance is seen clearly in Genesis 6 where God held the world accountable for its rebellion while righteous "Noah found grace in the eyes of the Lord." Noah offers a stunning example. Even in a world where "every intention of the thoughts of his [humanity's] heart was only evil continually" (Gen 6:5), Noah maintained the ability to choose righteousness—and God chose to notice.

Deuteronomy 6:1–9 documents that God's truth is both knowable and teachable. The remainder of that chapter promises that God holds people accountable.

Joshua 24:14ff is well-known to most students of the Bible. We can choose—we are compelled to choose—whom we will serve. Micah 6:8 asks the great question, "What does the Lord require of you?" The language of obligation and responsibility is frequent in Scripture.

As we help others toward spiritual health and wholeness, we're blessed to remember the balanced teaching of Ezekiel 18. God promises to judge "every one according to his ways" (Ezek 18:30). "The soul who sins shall die. The son shall not suffer for the iniquity of the father, nor the father suffer for the iniquity of the son" (Ezek 18:20). In even the closest of family relationships, the principle of individual responsibility still applies. In even the most challenging of situations, it continues to apply (Ezek 33).

Another aspect of understanding personal responsibility is recognizing that, while all of us are affected by our genetics and our environment, genetics are not the only factor. A just and righteous man can beget a son who robs, kills, and oppresses. While not the norm (Prov 22:6), it happens. On the blessed side, the son of a rebel is not doomed to rebellion. Evil Manasseh was Hezekiah's son. Righteous Jonathan was Saul's son. DNA does not determine destiny, even in a physical sense. Our choices and God's blessings still come into play.

As church leaders who attempt to help others, we are not responsible for the decisions made by others. Our responsibility lies in faithful teaching, warning, and effort. We know this is true, but when people we love make bad choices, we still feel terrible. There's major blessing in examining those feelings. We're unwise to let them cause false guilt—feelings of guilt over outcomes we never wanted, fought to prevent, and could not control.

A sixth aspect of wellness is recognizing that we are able to be proactive and self-determining rather than reactive. The famous playground version goes like this:

Parent: "Why did you punch Johnny?"

Child: "I had no choice; he punched me first."

As parents, we see the error of narrowmindedness. We see the false assertion. Your kid didn't have to punch back. He could have come to you for help. He could have gone to Johnny's mom. He could have walked away. He could have asked any available adult to intervene. Learning to see those options and having the courage and judgment to choose well is part of growing up. Unfortunately, some people don't grow up.

2 Samuel 16 offers a stunning example. Absalom has rebelled. In fear and shame, David flees from Jerusalem. As he escapes, Shimei, a relative of Saul, publicly curses him. He falsely announces that God is judging David for the bloody end of Saul's reign. He even throws stones at the king and his soldiers.

David's man, Abishai, wants to end this abuse. He asks permission to remove Shimei's head. David rebukes this offer in the most faithful of ways: "Leave him alone, and let him curse, for the Lord has told him to. It may be that the Lord will look on the wrong done to me and that the Lord will repay me with good for his cursing today" (2 Sam 16:11–12). What a stunning foreshadowing of Romans 12:17–21! Act better than you feel. Extend grace and mercy, even when they're undeserved. Don't meet sin at its own level. Learn what you can from the situation. Trust God to make things right.

1 Peter 2:18–25 offers strong teaching as well:

> For to this you have been called, because Christ also suffered for you, leaving you an example, so that you might follow in His steps. He committed no sin, neither was deceit found in His mouth. When He was reviled, He did not revile in return, when He suffered, He did not threaten, but continued entrusting Himself to Him who judges justly.

As we sing, "He could have called 10,000 angels to destroy the world and set Him free." He chose the stunningly higher road, and He calls on us to do the same.

Many people believe that in times of threat and danger there is a direct link between action and reaction. They are mistaken. Between action and reaction is some degree of decision making, some degree of processing, no matter how rudimentary. Part of spiritual maturity is making sure that processing is godly rather than thoughtless or selfless. We see examples of such godly wellness in both Acts 5:41, where the apostles "left the presence of the council, rejoicing that they were counted worthy to suffer dishonor for the name" and Hebrews 10:34, where the Hebrew Christians "joyfully accepted the plundering of your [their] property" out of loyalty to Christ. Knowing and serving Jesus changes everything.

A seventh evidence of spiritual wellness is maintaining a proper balance between temporal and eternal concerns. "In the beginning God created the heavens and the earth" (Gen 1:1). "The earth is the Lord's and the fullness thereof" (Ps 24:1). "The heavens declare the glory of God, and the sky above proclaims His handiwork" (Ps 19:1). At the same time, sin horribly damaged God's creation. "Therefore whoever wishes to be a friend of the world makes himself an enemy of God" (Jas 4:4).

> Do not love the things of the world or the things that are in the world. If anyone loves the world, the love of the Father is not in him. For all that is in the world—the desires of the flesh and the desires of the eyes and pride in possessions—is not from the Father but is from the world (1 John 2:15–16).

On top of that, even the better aspects of this world, being temporal, will pass away (1 Tim 6:6–7, 2 Pet 3:10–12). We can take nothing material from this world, but Christians can "lay up treasures in heaven" (Matt 6:19–21). We can teach ourselves and others "to do good, to be rich in good works, to be generous and ready to share, thus shoring up for themselves a good foundation for the future, so that they may take hold of that which is truly life" (1 Tim 6:18–19).

What a blessing to be able to engage life here with optimism and gratitude while knowing our best life lies in God's tomorrow! We can care for the plant, work to feed our families, and enjoy the beauties of nature, knowing that eternal joy and the indescribable beauties of heaven await. And when life is at its most challenging, we turn to 2 Corinthians 4:16–5:11 for perspective: "For this light momentary affliction is preparing for us an eternal weight of glory beyond all comparison" (1 Cor

4:17). That's why "we walk by faith not by sight" (1 Cor 5:7).

Our values, priorities, and sacrifices make no sense if there is no God, no judgment, and no heaven. If God, judgment, heaven, and hell are real, our loyalty to Jesus is worth more than life itself.

A final aspect of wellness is choosing to maintain a healthy sense of belonging and connectedness with others. The one God of the Bible reveals Himself in eternal perfect relationship. We understand "Let Us make man in Our image, after Our likeness" to speak of God the Father, God the Son, and God the Spirit (Gen 1:26). We are well reminded that all of God's creation was good except "it is not good that the man should be alone" (Gen 2:18). We love the powerful reminder of Ecclesiastes 4:9–11; in so many circumstances, "two are better than one." Jesus sent the twelve and the seventy two by two (Mark 6:7, Luke 10:1). When the church was born, "God added to their number day by day those who were being saved" (Acts 2:47). The togetherness of the first Christians is amazing (Acts 2:42–47). The Holy Spirit called Barnabas and Saul as the first mission team (Acts 13:2). Paul's mission efforts continually involved a team of servants.

Though we'd never deny that a Christian can be faithful alone in a prison cell or on a deserted island, we recognize the power and wisdom of the "one another" aspect of life in Christ. Bluntly, we need one another. We're better together in Christ. The God who called us to Christ through the gospel has always known that.

The line below has helped us think about wellness in terms of belonging and connectedness to others. Please think of "extreme dependence" and "extreme independence" as undesirable, impractical, and unbiblical. Please think of "interdependence" as godly and blessed, the healthy balance between two dangers. To be well and stay well, we need God and one another. The more well we are, the stronger our spiritual health and the stronger our ability to help others. Through God's goodness, the more we help others God's way, the healthier we'll become.

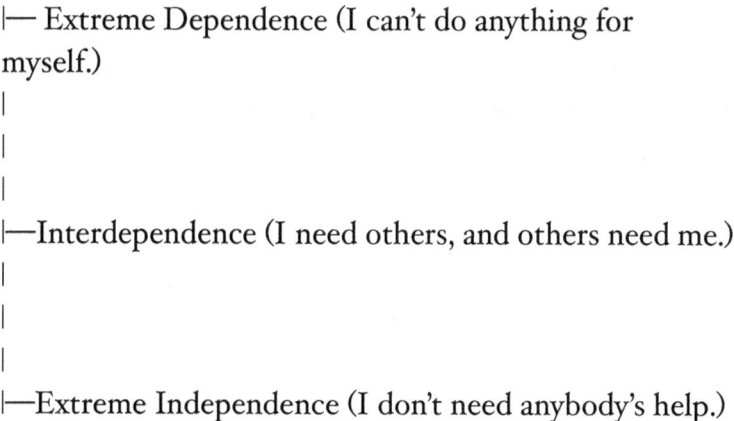

CHAPTER 3
WHAT SHOULD & SHOULDN'T SCARE PEOPLE ABOUT COUNSELING

"I'm afraid it's cancer." "I'm afraid it will rain." "I'm afraid my child is addicted to drugs." "I'm afraid to bungee jump." "I'm afraid — ," a phrase we hear quite often completed by a variety of rational and irrational triggers. Fear is a God-given emotion and can motivate us, protect us, and help us make wise decisions. Fear can also paralyze us, cause us to make poor choices, or put our spiritual, emotional, or physical well-being in jeopardy. In chapter 12 we will have an in-depth discussion of fear/worry/anxiety, but for our purposes in this chapter, let's just operate with the understanding there are some things we need to fear and some things we don't. Some of our concerns are rational and fact-based, some are not.

When you read the title of this chapter, it may not be clear to you if we are talking about being scared of going to counseling or fear of being in the role of counselor. Since we assume you are reading this book to help prepare you to minister to others by providing counsel, we will discuss the topic from the prospective of being a counselor. However, we do want to acknowledge that many people have concerns about going to counseling. You may need to address or acknowledge those concerns with those you are trying to help. They may fear embarrassment, judgment, vulnerability, or a variety of other concerns when they come to you for help. We hope that by good practice of confidentiality, empathy, and active listening, you will alleviate those fears.

What scares you about counseling? How do you know if your concerns are justified or just the devil whispering in your ear, causing you to doubt yourself and limiting your effectiveness in ministry? While the list of concerns varies as much as the personalities and skills of the readers of this book, we will attempt to identify and elucidate some of the more common concerns. If you have additional concerns, please find a knowledgeable person to help clarify those issues. Of course the most innocent of actions or words have the potential of creating a firestorm, so thoughtful processing prior to enacting or speaking is always wise (James 1:19).

ISSUE #1: "I DON'T KNOW ENOUGH TO HELP ANYBODY. I'M AFRAID I'LL SAY THE WRONG THING."

The most dangerous counselor is the one who thinks he has all the answers. The most thoroughly trained and highly educated counselor does not always know the right thing to say. As we discuss counseling in the following chapters, we will emphasize the counseling skills that facilitate a client's ability to explore and problem-solve. Advice giving (or telling someone what to do to solve his or her problem) is not the purpose of counseling. In counseling, you want Jesus to be your example of skillful questioning and, when appropriate, challenging. The goal is to help the client develop skills to problem-solve, not only the presenting problem, but also difficult issues that will arise in the future. When you are in the role of counselor, please keep in mind your client knows the problem and the intricacies of his or her life so much better than what you know from your outsider assessment. Your client, with your assistance, is in a much better position to know what is possible or doable as he/she works to resolve the problem. It's possible to get lost in the fog of the problem; it is your role to help him or her find the way to successful living.

In responding to a client's questions or presentation of the problem at hand, you will find yourself relying on two unfailing resources. First is scripture:

> All Scripture is breathed out by God and profitable for teaching, for reproof, for correction, and for training in righteousness, that the man of God may be complete, equipped for every good work (2 Tim 3:16–17).

As you talk with clients, scriptures will come to mind. There may also be topics that you will need to study and explore along with your client to seek and understand God's will on that subject and related issues according to scripture.

The second resource actually has two parts intricately woven together: prayer and the Holy Spirit. Pray before, during, and after counseling sessions. Seek guidance for yourself as you help others. Then get out of the way and allow God's Spirit to lead you in what to say and do. There are hundreds of counseling methods currently in use. In *Christian Counseling: a Comprehensive Guide*, Gary Collins states,

> There seems to be as many theories and approaches to counseling as there are counselors. With all this advice and activity, even full-time professionals can feel overwhelmed.[1]

Jesus, the Counselor, used a variety of counseling techniques. The type of problem, the situation, and the nature or disposition of the client influenced His approach. Jesus promised the presence of the Holy Spirit to guide and comfort us. We are not saying the Holy Spirit will take control of your mouth and cause you to utter words beyond your control or knowledge. However, the Spirit will help you listen, gain insight, and guide your clients as you exhibit in your counsel the fruits of the Spirit: love, joy, peace, patience, kindness, goodness, faithfulness, gentleness, and self-control (Gal 5:22–23).

With all of this in mind, you remain a flawed human and will still sometimes "say the wrong thing." You will not have the perfect response to every situation.

Recognizing you have made a mistake gives you the opportunity to model for your client what Christians do when they have erred. (1) Acknowledge the mistake, (2) apologize, (3) ask for forgiveness (if appropriate), and (4) try again—rephrase, take a detour, or regroup. Do not let the mistake get you off track from helping the client. Do not let the session become about you. Move on and refocus on the client. Show your client the love of Christ (1 John 4:21, 1 Pet 4:8), and God will be glorified through your counseling.

ISSUE #2: "I'M AFRAID I'LL GET SUED."

Laws in each country, state, or province regulate the professional practice of counseling. It is strongly recommended that you check the *current* laws and statutes of the state in which you reside or counsel. Likewise, you must become familiar with guidelines in any foreign country where you are acting in the role of counselor in a mission or outreach effort. These laws would govern licensure and competency in the professional practice of counseling. (If you are not engaging in the professional practice of counseling, these laws would not apply to you.) As you plan for your ministry and your availability to help others through compassionate, problem solving conversation, it is paramount that you portray yourself as who and what you are: an elder, deacon, ministry leader, caring friend, or Bible class teacher. You must NEVER overstate your qualifications or education as related to counseling. Also, if for example, you have a PhD in biology and are known in your work setting or even socially as "Doctor Smith," you may not use that title in a counseling setting. When counseling members of your congregation or others in an outreach effort, you should inform or remind the client that you have no degree in counseling, but you can also tell him or her what does qualify you to counsel. You can share, for example, that you love God and you love the client and his or her family. You can let clients know you want to help them have a happy and peaceful life on earth, and ultimately to have a home in heaven.

There are some things that could make you vulnerable to lawsuit or legal action, but they are not related to your expertise or skill as a counselor. The actions or behaviors that make you vulnerable to legal problems would be the same things that make you vulnerable in everyday life. Assault, harassment, exploitation, abuse, or inappropriate sexual behavior or speech can all get you in trouble regardless of the setting, but are especially egregious in a church related counseling setting.

The American Psychological Association (APA), the American Counseling Association (ACA), and the American Association of Christian Counselors (AACC) all have published ethical guidelines that might be interesting reading for you. These would be posted on each organization's website. The AACC Code of Ethics would be most inline with the type of counseling done in a ministry setting. Following is an excerpt from the AACC Code of Ethics.

> 4-120: Rules of Ethics Code Application and Exemption
>
> Lay caregivers and non-ordained ministers—by law and/or regulation—are not typically required or held to the same standard of professional conduct as licensed practitioners. Nevertheless, they recognize possible moral and/or ethical imperatives that may still exist as part of a Judeo-Christian ethic.[2]

So the bottom line of this section is, you do not need to be hyper-concerned about being sued for malpractice in counseling, but you do need to behave morally and ethically.

ISSUE #3: "I CAN'T HELP SOMEONE ELSE WHEN MY OWN LIFE IS FAR FROM PERFECT."

This scene has been replayed several times.
The phone rings.
Me: Hello, this is Rosemary Snodgrass.
Caller: I'm calling about marriage counseling.
Me: Okay. We can set up an appointment for you and your spouse.
Caller: Well, I have some questions before I make an appointment.
Me: Okay. What would you like to ask?
Caller: Are you married?
Me: Yes.
Caller: How long have you been married?
Me: About 40 years. (Of course that number changed during the course of my career).
Caller: To the same man!?!?
Me: Yes.
Caller: Then I'd like to make an appointment.

In the many times this question has been asked, I've never had anyone ask about the degree of happiness in my marriage. I guess perseverance has some merit. I've had other potential clients ask if I have children, if I've been a drug addict (by the way, that answer is "no"), if

I've experienced the death of a loved one, and about other life situations. I have had more questions of a personal nature than inquiries about my education, licensure, or therapeutic approach.

Several years ago I heard Coach Gene Stallings speak at Mars Hill Bible School in Florence, Alabama. In that speech he mentioned that while he was still coaching, former players would call to ask to come back and tell the college players not to make the mistakes they made while in college—don't use drugs, don't be promiscuous, don't get caught up in the party life. Coach Stallings said he would tell the caller that he appreciated his call and he was very happy he had straightened out his life, but he didn't need him to come speak to the players. Coach Stallings explained to the audience why he would decline their offers. He wanted his players to hear from young men who had faced those same temptations but avoided the pitfalls. He wanted someone who could tell the players how to succeed.

While I agree with Coach Stallings, I do also see the benefit of previous experience in some situations. If someone has failed to avoid the pitfall, it could be beneficial to hear encouragement from someone who went down that path but has corrected his course. The person who has failed needs to know that change is possible. Isn't that at the core of being a Christian? "For all have sinned and fall short of the glory of God, and are justified by his grace as a gift, through the redemption that is in Christ Jesus" (Rom 3:23–24).

If we limit helping others to only those who have lived flawlessly, where would we find anyone qualified? Of course, flawed people can help other flawed people.

Remember that in counseling, you are helping the client discover how to navigate a better course in his or her life. It is possible your own life experiences could limit your ability to help others if (1) you are so distracted by a current problem that it limits your ability to attend to your client, or (2) the problem of a client is so similar to a personal problem you have experienced that it conjures up an emotional response that interferes with your ability to be objective about the client's problem. If either of these situations occurs, you should refer the client to someone else for counseling.

ISSUE #4: "I'M AFRAID TO TALK TO SOMEONE WHO IS SUICIDAL. WHAT IF SOMEONE COMMITTED SUICIDE AFTER TALKING WITH ME? HOW COULD I LIVE WITH THAT?"

The most recent data reported by the Centers for Disease Control and Prevention indicate that in 2018, more than 48,000 people committed suicide in the United States. Despite efforts of many organizations and agencies to raise awareness and educate, the suicide rate increased by 35% from 1999 to 2018.[3] SAMHSA, a division of the U.S. Department of Health and Human Services, reports that during 2019 in the United States, twelve million adults had serious thoughts of suicide.[4]

The numbers indicate there is a very good possibility that you will be called on to help someone with suicidal ideation or someone concerned for a family member who is considering suicide, has attempted suicide, or has committed suicide. When faced with this situation, remember that you do not have control over anyone else's behavior. What you say will not determine the outcome of the situation. God gave His human creation free will. Do not be afraid to ask if a client is contemplating suicide. Many helpers fear to ask a client about suicidal thoughts for fear the client will take the probe as a suggestion. This fear is unfounded. Getting suicidal ideation out in the open allows for rational discussion of the consequences and impact of the individual's suicide. When talking to a suicidal client, the most important consideration when talking to a suicidal client is safety; the client's safety of course, but also the safety of those around the suicidal client as well as your own safety. All too often we see the headlines about a murder-suicide event. Be sure to protect others and yourself.

ISSUE #5: "I DON'T WANT TO GET INVOLVED IN LEGAL BATTLES. I'M AFRAID TO TESTIFY IN COURT."

Other than lawyers, very few people WANT to get involved in court or legal battles. The main thing to remember if called to testify is simple—"tell the truth, the whole truth, and nothing but the truth." Generally, it is best to answer the questions that are asked without volunteering additional information. Do not express opinions or assumptions unless asked. If a personal opinion is requested, it will probably be met with an objection from the opposing counsel. Do not take it personally when lawyers "argue" their case—it's what they are paid to do.

We can try to make a legal plea to be exempt from

testifying in court on the basis of "a minister acting in a professional capacity as a spiritual advisor." In churches of Christ there are no "ordained" or "credentialed pastors." If the client sees us in the role of a "minister acting in a professional capacity," it is *possible* the judge will uphold the client's right to confidentiality based on the clergy-penitent privilege. For churches that have ordained pastors, it may be difficult for a non-ordained church member to claim this exemption. If a client wants us to testify on his or her behalf, we have no claim to clergy privilege and would be obligated to testify. For those involved in marriage counseling, it is a legal gray area as to whether ministers can be compelled to testify without consent of both parties in order to testify in court.

ISSUE #6: ETHICS/CONFIDENTIALITY

As a non-professional counselor, you are not bound to the ethical guidelines and the obligation of confidentiality that are in place for professional counselors. However, as noted earlier in the Code of Ethics of the American Association of Christian Counselors 4-120: Rules of Ethics Code Application and Exemption, there is an expectation of lay-counselors to behave in a moral and ethical manner, including keeping information shared in counseling confidential.[5] If you hope to be an effective helper, you must avoid disclosing information shared with you in a counseling conversation. The simple fact that you are in a counseling relationship with an individual should be kept confidential. It is vital to your success in helping to have the trust of church members and others that information shared with you will be treated with respect and kept confidential.

ISSUE #7: INAPPROPRIATE RELATIONSHIP

A counseling relationship is an intimate relationship. During a counseling session, very personal information can be shared, and clients may feel extremely vulnerable. For an effective counseling relationship to exist, there must be a great deal of trust between the helper and the one being helped. Because of this intimacy, sharing, vulnerability, and trust; the client can become very attached and dependent in the counselor-client relationship. For an emotionally fragile client, the intimacy involved in this relationship can be very confusing. It is the responsibility of the counselor to maintain appropriate boundaries and to clearly maintain appropriate physical and emotional distance between client and counselor.

Unfortunately, there are those times when the helper fails to maintain appropriate boundaries. Counselors have emotional needs too. They desire to be helpful to others, and when the client expresses appreciation for help and admiration for the counselor, it can become a very dangerous situation if not handled appropriately. Often we think of inappropriate relationships of a sexual or romantic type, but there are other inappropriate relationships. Counseling a friend can lead to a loss of objectivity on the part of the counselor. Sometimes a business relationship could interfere with effective counseling. Any type of *quid pro quo* arrangement would also be inappropriate. Several things can be done to avoid these pitfalls, and they will be discussed in more detail in our chapter on Avoiding Traps.

ISSUE #8: "I WAS JUST TRYING TO HELP. SHE DIDN'T TELL ME SHE WAS MENTALLY ILL."

As church leaders we will encounter people who have a serious mental illness (SMI). The National Institute for Mental Health reported in 2019 that 5.2% of the adult population in the United States suffers from an SMI.[6] Those individuals will not always be obvious to us. Many people with an SMI are functioning effectively with the help of medication and intervention, but they can also get off track. Failure to take medication, a physiological change triggering a need to adjust medication, or a change in circumstances may make a previous dose of medication inadequate so that the person's level of functioning suffers.

The rational, stable person we have known may change. Their behavior may become erratic, their thinking irrational, or they may become a danger to self or others. As a helper, it is important for you to recognize when a person is suffering an SMI episode. It is equally important to realize that SMI is beyond the scope of our ability to help. The best we can do is assist getting the individual the needed help. Depending on the situation, the help can come from various sources. SMI intervention requires extensive training and credentialing you do not possess as a non-professional. In many cases the ability to prescribe medication is necessary. If the person's thinking and reasoning is so distorted that he or she is not capable of making rational decisions, the family or other concerned people can seek legal advice to have the individual declared incompetent. Laws vary from state to state, so we would need to become familiar with the laws where we are trying to help.

Though we have talked about the importance of confidentiality, the exception to that would be if we believe someone to be a danger to self or others. Safety demands we take action to protect our client and others. This may mean notifying a family member, getting the client to the hospital, or calling the police, depending on the volatility of the situation.

ISSUE #9: "SHE SAID HER HUSBAND HAD A GUN, BUT I THOUGHT I COULD HELP CALM THEM DOWN."

Police officers will say that the most dangerous encounters they have are domestic violence situations. When someone reaches a point where he or she is willing to inflict harm to a loved one, rational thinking is no longer happening. Our presence may exacerbate the situation rather than bring calm. If a person says his/her spouse is hurting him/her, the first priority is to accept what we have been told. We must accept it enough to recognize it as a volatile situation. Because of the potential for harm, steps need to be taken to ensure the safety of all involved. If the spouse is in pursuit, then lock the doors and call law enforcement. Do not try to intervene or reason with a person who is irrational. Later there will be time—in a calm, safe environment—to sort out exactly what has happened. Allow the police to use their training to defuse the situation and get everyone in a safe location. Most communities have shelters for women, and some have facilities for men who are in danger of harm from their spouses. If the danger is not imminent, we could assist the one seeking help to make contact with a protective shelter. We need to remember: By trying to shelter someone in this situation, we could be putting ourselves, our family, our co-workers, and possibly other innocent people in harm's way. Help, but help wisely and safely. Do not try to be a hero.

Do not be afraid to help others by giving them the opportunity to talk with a caring Christian. But we must be wise in our efforts. As Paul taught Timothy, "God gave us a spirit not of fear but of power and love and self-control" (2 Tim 1:7).

Endnotes

[1] Gary R. Collins, *Christian Counseling: A Comprehensive Guide,* rev. ed. (Dallas: Word Publishing, 1988), 15.
[2] https://www.aacc.net/wp-content/uploads/2017/10/AACC-Code-of-Ethics-Master-Document.pdf
[3] Center for Disease Control and Prevention, NCHS Data Brief No. 362, April 2020. http://www.cdc.gov.
[4] Substance Abuse and Mental Health Services Association, *Help Prevent Suicide.* 10/7/2020. http://www.SAMHSA.gov.
[5] The American Association of Christian Counselors, *Code of Ethics.* http://www.aacc.net.
[6] National Institute of Mental Health, *Mental Health Information: Statistics.* http://www.nimh.nih.gov.

CHAPTER 4

WHY DO PEOPLE SEEK COUNSELING?

People seek counseling for many diverse reasons, some of which they don't even realize. Everyone who has done much people-helping has heard a version of the following: "I'm sorry to bother you. I know you probably can't help me. I don't even know why I've come!" What are we to think when we hear such pain, lament, courage, honesty, and uncertainty?

For church leaders, a great initial thought flows from Esther 4:14: "And who knows whether you have not come to the kingdom for such a time as this?" Has God put us here today to address this need? To help this person? To serve with compassion in the name of Jesus? To save a life? To save a family? To protect or save a soul? To learn something that will help us help others with more skill and confidence in the future? Has God providentially led them to us because He knows that we are able to help? Have they chosen us because they've seen something of Jesus in us (Acts 4:13)?

It's our conviction that God is the author of everything good, including the opportunity to serve in His name (Jas 1:17). It's our conviction that God is the ultimate multitasker; He is able work on countless levels at once. When someone comes to us for help, God can use us as instruments of His grace (Eph 4:29). We're honored to serve in His name. As we're helping, we're also learning and growing on multiple levels. We discover more of the depth, breadth, and power of God's word. We discover talents God has given us that were previously hidden from our understanding. And we discover more of our weaknesses and limitations. We learn that so much lies beyond our understanding, our ability, and our control. We learn to pray better, we learn to manage our expectations, and we learn to be more humble. Have they come because God is using them to help us?

To be optimistic, there's a compliment in being asked to help in time of pain, struggle, or crisis. They trusted us enough to reach out. They chose us in their moment of need. Please accept that compliment. We'll need the encouragement it brings to find the heart to keep helping the hurting. The joy and energy from each positive prepare us to face the next set of challenges.

On the flip side, people sometimes come to church leaders for help because they hope we're both softhearted and soft-headed. They come not only for understanding, but for validation. They want us to agree with decisions they've already made or actions they've already taken, even if those actions and decisions aren't biblical. Not to be rude, but it's like King Saul trying to con Samuel in 1 Samuel 15. If only Samuel will listen to the king's explanation, then he'll understand. He'll soften his tone and get onboard. Adam also attempted this approach in Genesis 3.

There's a worse version of this reason: Sometimes people come to church leaders for counseling because they want absolution. They have violated both God's commandment and their consciences. The guilt is killing them. Often, they rightly fear God's judgment. They won't use these words, but their message is, "I know I've done wrong, and it's tearing me up. Please tell me that what I've done is okay." As godly leaders we must speak the truth in love (Eph 4:15), but we must speak only truth. Only godly sorrow works repentance (2 Cor 7:2–12). Feeling bad and being comforted by a church leader is not a remedy for sin.

THREE ADDITIONAL BASER REASONS

Bluntly, sometimes people come to church leaders for counseling because they can't afford "a real counselor." Free services are rare. The services of mental health professionals aren't cheap. It's a test of humility to hear, "I guess I need to be honest. I wouldn't be here if I could afford to be somewhere else." If the devil could sit on our shoulder in such a moment, he'd say, "Throw them out! Who needs another insult?" We must not allow our hearts to listen to such language. Instead of feeling insulted, we could choose to express appreciation for their honest expression of reluctance. We could choose to mark that honesty as an anchor point from which we can begin to help. Compliment their honesty and courage. Then, recognize that it takes mature love on our part to say, "I'm glad you're here anyway. How can I help?"

Sometimes people come to church leaders for counseling because they're being forced to come. Think of a teen who drank, drove, and wrecked his car. The parents mandate counseling with an elder or trusted teacher. "You will talk to ___, or else!" Think of a wife who has endured neglect (or worse) for a decade. She says to her husband, "You will talk with someone at church this week, or I'm filing for divorce." Sometimes people seek our help because they have few options and we're the least bad option.

There's an art to talking with people who don't want to talk with you. Our first recommendation is Do NOT ignore the elephant in the room. What does that look like? "Thank you for being here today to talk. I know you don't want to be here, but you are. Since you're here, we have options. We can sit in silence, we can go through the motions and check off the box, or we can see if there's something we might do to be of help." There's power in choosing to face the elephant in the room. There's amazing power in giving hurting people the right to choose their next action. Given both honesty and a set of choices, an impressive number of people choose well.

Sometimes people come to church leaders for counseling because they have something to hide. They recognize that we're not mental health professionals. We'd be easier to fool. We apologize if this sounds jaded. Happily, it's not frequent. Regrettably, it's also not rare. Everyone who tries to help people will get fooled upon occasion. There are people more skilled at deception than we are at detection. Most deceivers aren't that skilled. Look for consistency and congruence. Does the narrative being presented have the ring of truth? Does it make sense? If not, ask for clarification. Don't just pretend that everything is okay. We must trust our eyes. "Even a child makes himself known by his acts, by whether his conduct is pure and upright" (Prov 20:11).

THREE DANGERS

Some people come to church leaders for help because they want quick, easy, and painless answers. As church leaders, we know and serve God. We can call on God for help. God can do anything—the Bible says so. "And I tell you, ask, and it will given to you, seek, and you will find, knock, and it will be opened to you" (Luke 11:9). "Therefore, confess your sins to one another and pray for one another, that you may be healed. The prayer of a righteous person has great power as it is working" (Jas 5:16). The untaught—and people in pain—often read verses in isolation, failing to consider the broader teaching of Scripture.

A modern proverb of unknown origin states, "For every complex problem, there is an answer that is simple, easy, and wrong." We find that proverb brilliant. As a rule, problems created over decades can't be solved in days. Even hurts that can be healed often leave scars. Some situations are intractable—they have no full solution in this life because a full solution would require the repentance and cooperation of multiple people, some of whom are dead. Think of Jesus's prayer in Gethsemane (Matt 26) or Paul's prayer in 2 Corinthians 12. Both were heartfelt, but neither was answered in a quick, easy, or painless manner.

Some people come to church leaders for counseling because doing so accrues less stigma than going to a mental health professional. Thankfully, the stigma of seeking counseling has declined in a major way in the US. Most people don't fear being labeled as weak, crazy, or mentally ill. Sadly, a degree of stigma still exists, especially among conservative religious groups. Therein, the stigma is both broader and deeper. Seeking counseling, especially from a source outside the church, is labeled by some as lack of faith in God or lack of appreciation for grace.

We urge church leaders to assist in destigmatizing counseling on every level. Seeking needed help is a sign of strength rather than weakness, evidence of faith and hope rather than fear and despair. It can mean much when we commend those who seek our assistance.

Some request help from church leaders because of fear. They hate the damaging decisions that litter their past. They have listened to family members or others and been harmed. Their lives are plagued by anxiety and uncertainty. Sometimes the fearful need a strong dose of education (Phil 4:4–9). Sometimes they need an extended, wise, and compassionate dose of comfort (1 Thess 5:14). But there's more.

Some fearful people seek far too much help from their church leaders. At the extreme, they'd love to have us take over their lives. "Just tell me what to do, and I'll do it. Anything you say, I promise, it's as good as done." We must recognize the trap. None of us are wise or knowledgeable enough to take over another person's life.

Even if we were, we'd be wrong to do so. We help people shoulder, not avoid, responsibility (Prov 16:32, 20:11, & 25:28; Ezek 18; 2 Cor 5:9–11). We help people grow up, not remain perpetually immature (Eph 4:11–16, Col 3:12–17, 2 Pet 1:5–8).

A DEVELOPMENTAL PERSPECTIVE

One of the great divides regarding why people seek counseling is developmental vs. situational needs. Situational needs/reasons flow from events, particularly crises. People often seek counseling when there's an unexpected pregnancy, a job loss, an illness, or a death—a traumatic life event. They were functioning well prior to this overloading event, and their request for help flows directly from this troubling situation.

Developmental needs flow primarily from pressures and changes at predictable stages of life. Think of moving away to college, marriage, first baby, career change, having a child move away, purchasing or building a house, moving to a different city for a job promotion, declining health of parents, death of parents, etc. Church leaders could benefit from a study of developmental stages. Developmental theories aren't gospel, but they offer priceless insights. Often, those seeking our help in such times have the same fundamental questions: "Is this normal?" "Am I normal?" We're reminded of the ancient book, *Normal Is a Setting on Your Dryer*.

Humor aside, "normal" covers a very broad range. There can be enormous comfort in being able to tell a person who faces a developmental crisis, "What you are facing, while important and concerning, is just as normal as can be. Many people face the needs and questions that you have expressed today." Often, after such a statement, good people respond, "Whew! You don't know how much better I feel. I was afraid I was the only one." We're not denying individuality; rather, we're affirming our common humanity. It often helps just to know that we're not alone in our struggles.

Brethren may seek our help because they need an objective opinion. They have studied, prayed, and thought. They have done their best to humble themselves under God's hand and cast their care on Him (1 Pet 5:6). From a human perspective, they have weighed options and attempted cost/benefit analysis. Now, they want to check their thinking through a trusted, spiritual friend. "Have I missed anything?" "Is my thinking sound?" "What else do I need to consider?"

There's another developmental reason that leads some to seek the help of church leaders. They read 2 Timothy 3:14–17 and focus on Paul's teaching that God's word is profitable and equipping. They want to be better listeners, better teachers, and better communicators. They want to be better parents, better friends, and better Christians. They believe God's word can help them in countless practical ways, and they want church leaders to help them claim these gifts. Such personal growth is outstandingly encouraging when it's sought to make us better servants of God.

On another spiritual level, some insightful Christians seek spiritual counsel upon reading Ephesians 4:11–16 and realizing that their level of spiritual maturity and stability isn't as strong as they wish. They want to be closer to God. They want to be more like Jesus. None of us have in every sense grown "up in every way into him who is the head, into Christ" (Eph 4:13). What a sweet, humbling, and sacred opportunity to help spiritual seekers become more spiritual! When brethren seek spiritual mentoring, that both humbles and blesses us. We are moved to acknowledge our imperfection, but we're also called to step up in the spirit of 1 Corinthians 11:1, 16:15–16; and Philippians 3:17.

FEAR OF OTHER SOURCES OF HELP

Sometimes brethren seek the help of church leaders because they fear secular counselors. Some have endured negative experiences. Others have heard warnings from family, friends, and church leaders. We cannot deny that some secular counselors exhibit varying degrees of hostility toward religion. Secular, even atheistic, mental health professionals continue to enhance our understanding of wellness and good function. One need not be Freudian or endorse all his values to appreciate the brilliance of recognizing the unconscious and the deployment of defense mechanisms.

What's a church leader to do with this knowledge of the mixture of danger and blessing with secular counselors? An initial recommendation is to employ the Fish/Bones Principle. Within any profession, practice, or literature, that which accords with Scripture is fish. Benefit from it. Anything that contradicts Scripture is bones. Discard the bones. It's one thing to state the principle; it's far superior to model and teach it.

A second recommendation is to avoid extremism in any form. We shouldn't say more than we know. Don't lump everyone into meaninglessly broad categories. Appreciate all that should be appreciated, and warn against anything dangerous to the soul.

A third recommendation is to build a safe referral list. When a person requests our help and we know that the need is beyond our ability, to whom can we refer? Our first choice always is a fellow Christian who has the skills and knowledge. Second choice would be a person who exhibits values that are consistent with biblical teachings. Our never-ever choice would be a person known to attack and undermine faith in God.

A RELATED QUESTION

Under what conditions and for what reasons should we, as church leaders, offer counsel to others? The reasons were partially covered in the introduction. We offer help because God has demonstrated His love toward us (Rom 5:5–8), because Christ commands us to love (John 13:34–35), because of the Golden Rule (Matt 7:12), because we are our brother's keeper, because it's part of being a decent human (Luke 10:25–37), because we believe God will help us as we help others (Gal 6:6–10), because we want the church to be strong (Phil 2:1–4), because we want families to be blessed, because we love to reduce suffering, and because we want to help others toward heaven.

From a different perspective, we help because we can. We help because if we don't the world might, but the world's help will come with destructive strings. We help because the people around us need help. We help because even the unchurched know that churches are supposed to help people.

Under what conditions do church leaders offer counseling help to others? Certainly, we help all who request our help, including those who even informally hint as asking. Requests need not be formal or overt. We help as God opens doors of opportunity. Because God is ever aware and always good, we assume that any hint of an opportunity is a gift from God to be lovingly pursued. Sometimes requests for help come indirectly, from a friend or family member.

A word of warning: Those who choose to help others in the name of Jesus, will quickly gain a reputation. If we are blessed to help others, those who need help will find us. Servants of God neither announce their good deeds nor act to be seen of men (Matt 6:1-18; Prov 27:2 and 25:27). At the same time, Matthew 5:13-16 applies. Good that brings glory to God cannot be hidden.

While helping people live in the joy of God's love is blessed and crucial work, we resist the temptation to become spiritual ambulance chasers. We respect people's choice, even when they delay addressing vital needs. We realize that we may be the smallest part of the team of helpers that God has in mind. He may use us to open hearts just a bit so that the next helper can do his/her part. When waiting is wise, we wait, no matter how difficult that is. Attempts to push and force almost always backfire. The pull of love remains far more powerful than the press of panic.

CHAPTER 5
THE BASICS OF LISTENING

"Know this, my beloved brothers: let every person be quick to hear, slow to speak" (James 1:19).

"When words are many, transgression is not lacking, but whoever restrains his lips is prudent" (Proverbs 10:19).

The Bible takes a very high view of listening. We're moved by the lament of Psalm 81:8, where God says, "O Israel, if you would listen to me," and 81:11, "But my people did not listen to my voice." The proverbs repeatedly appeal for listening ears (Prov 1:8–9 & 22, 8:32–36). We remember the famous statement of Jesus: "He who has ears to hear, let him hear" (Matt 11:15, 13:9, & 43; Rev 2:7, 11, 17, 29, & 3:6, 13, & 22). In perfect balance Jesus taught both "Pay attention to what you hear" (Mark 4:24) and "Take care then how you hear" (Luke 8:18). We note the action-guiding words of James that begin this chapter. And we know one major purpose of Proverbs 10:19; the person who speaks less has more time and energy for listening and learning.

GOD THE MASTER LISTENER

As part of its masterful revelation of the everlasting Creator, Scripture presents God the Father as the greatest of listeners. He has innumerable advantages over any human—including omniscience, perfect understanding, and perfect love. David beautifully states these truths in Psalm 139:1–4.

> O Lord, you have searched me and known me! You know when I sit down and when I rise up; you discern my thoughts from afar. You search out my path and my lying down and are acquainted with all my ways. Even before a word is on my tongue, behold, O Lord, you know it altogether.

David exalted God for His pre-understanding. Prayer—as supplication and confession—richly blesses all who pray in faith, but God knows our thoughts, needs, pains, and motives better than we do, even before we put them into words. We can never rightly say, "But God doesn't understand me!" While He graciously allows such cries of pain, He would have us know that those words cannot be true.

Scripture is replete with examples of God's skill in and heart for listening. Even after the fall, He initiated dialog with Adam and Eve and let them state their case (Gen 3:9–17). Fully knowing the sin and judgment of Sodom and Gomorrah, He patiently listened to Abraham's attempt at intercession (Gen 18:22–33). As Hagar and Ishmael faced death in the wilderness, "God heard the voice of the boy" (Gen 21:17) and intervened. Lest we miss the point, the phrase is repeated by the angel who came to help. God called Moses to deliver Israel from Egyptian bondage because "God heard their groaning" (Exod 2:24). God's word to Moses was, "I have surely seen the affliction of my people who are in Egypt and have heard their cry because of their taskmasters. I know their sufferings" (Exod 3:7). David extolled God's gracious listening in 2 Samuel 22:7: "In my distress I called upon the Lord; to my God I called. From his temple he heard my voice, and my cry came to his ears." Romans 8:26 beautifully implies Divine excellence in listening, teaching us that God the Spirit helps God the Father hear us more fully than we know how to speak. Amazing!

We would never claim to be able to match God's ability to care, listen, and understand. Still, we find His example both precious and compelling. Part of serving and being like God is following His example in listening.

THE LISTENING HEART

We often think of listening as a set of skills, and there is merit in such thinking. However, for Christians, listening flows from our character, from our commitment to imitate our loving God. We listen to hurting, needy, difficult, and struggling people because God listens to us. We listen because to listen is to love, and God is love (1 John 4:8).

Listening from a loving heart is selfless, humble, and

healing. It's also needed and powerful. It has strong biblical support. "So whatever you wish that others would do to you, do also to them, for this is the Law and the Prophets" (Matt 7:12). According to Jesus, selfless love summarizes and encapsulates the law God gave to Israel. Listening from the heart is universally recognized as an act of such love.

We listen because God has taught us to love one another (1 John 4:7–11). We listen because listening helps us battle self-centeredness. We listen because listening builds trust and heightens our ability to help others. We listen because helping others is central to our identity in Christ: "Do nothing from selfish ambition or conceit, but in humility count others more significant than yourselves. Let each of you look not only to his own interests, but also to the interests of others" (Phil 2:3–4).

We assert that following God's example of listening is spiritually formative. Repeated acts of loving listening will make our hearts more loving. Practicing godliness will make us more godly. Our actions shape our thinking and our character. We are confident that the Lord will never let us serve Him in vain. He will use our service to bless us, both in this world and in the world to come.

There are many verses in the Bible about the importance and the wisdom of listening more than we speak. In addition, Jesus shows us how skillful questioning and attentive listening lead to the development of relationships. In *Jesus, The Greatest Therapist Who Ever Lived*, Mark Baker writes,

> He [Jesus] knew that the highest form of knowledge comes not from amassing greater amounts of

information, but from trusting relationships. He answered direct questions with metaphors to invite listeners into a dialogue and into a relationship with him.[1]

As a church leader, a right relationship with Jesus is our ultimate goal for anyone we try to help. Dialogue and relationship are core components of effective counseling. The authors of *The Elements of Counseling* explain, "Counselors are skilled listeners. By learning about clients through attentive listening and offering acceptance of clients as they are, counselors develop a bond of trust and support."[2] Jesus provides us with examples of the power of attentive listening and relationship development. His discourse with the woman at the well (John 4:1–26) shows how His skillful questioning, unconditional love, and cultivation of a relationship bring about radical change in her life and in the lives of others. In John's record of the conversation between Jesus and the Samaritan woman, she makes six statements using 134 words, and in seven statements Jesus speaks 209 words. Of course we have no evidence that John recorded every word spoken in this conversation, but reaonably we can assume it was a fairly even dialogue that included questions and answers from both participants. Jesus listened to her and responded to her statements and questions. This is the type of conversation we need to have with those we are trying to help. We should strive to have a goal-oriented collaborative conversation, not a lecture or a sermon.

How should we go about establishing this therapeutic dialogue? The following suggestions can facilitate effective conversation.

1. No matter how well we know the people or the problem they are dealing with, we need to listen to them.

We need to listen to learn their perspective and understanding of the issues involved. Donald Rumsfeld was right when he said, "We don't know we don't know."[3] I think Mr. Rumsfeld was talking about terrorism, but it applies in many other situations as well. It definitely applies when trying to understand the thoughts, motivations, and actions of others. We can only speculate why someone acted as they did. What was their motivation? What were they thinking? Why did they behave that way?

Unlike us, Jesus knew everything about the woman at the well. After their conversation, she reported to the citizens of Sychar, "He told me all that I ever did" (John 4:39). Still, Jesus listened to her. He knew that relationships develop through communication. True dialogue requires a back-and-forth exchange of words. He listened to her to allow her to share her perspective on several topics. He knew we feel closer to people when we share our thoughts and feelings and they share with us.

2. Strive to have true dialogue.

Gerard Egan, a well-known counselor-educator and author, identifies four requirements for true dialogue. The first is **Turn Taking**. "You talk, then the other person talks. Helpers learn about their clients and base their interventions on what they come to understand through the give-and-take of the dialogue." Second is **Connecting**. "They (helper and client) need to actively listen to one another and respond in terms of what they think the other person is saying." The third part of true dialogue is **Mutual Influencing**. "In true dialogue the parties are open to being influenced by what the other person has to say. Helpers influence their clients, and open-minded helpers learn from and are influenced by their clients." The fourth element of true dialogue is **Co-creating Outcomes.**

> (C)ounseling is about results, accomplishments, and outcomes. The job of the counselor is neither to tell clients what to do nor merely to leave them to their own devices. The counselor's job is to act as a catalyst for the kind of problem-managing dialogue that helps clients find their own answers.[4]

During His dialogue with the Samaritan woman, Jesus showed us how to employ all of these characteristics of true dialogue.

3. Silence is golden.

In social settings silence can feel awkward, but in counseling it can be very helpful. "When you don't know what to say, say nothing,"[5] is the advice given by Meier and Davis. Silence gives clients an opportunity to process what has been said and to reflect on their lives and current situation. Silence also gives the helper time to process what has been said and to formulate the best way forward. A pause in the conversation will prompt clients to explore their thoughts and feelings, and a pause gives the helper time to formulate a good response to information their client shared. We don't just talk to fill the room with words because we feel uncomfortable with silence. On the negative side, silence could indicate the topic of the current conversation is too uncomfortable or painful for the client. In those cases, it may be advisable to back off and plan to revisit that topic at a later time—and possibly in a different way. It could also indicate the helper has misunderstood what the client was saying, but the client is hesitant to contradict or disagree with the counselor. During the silence, the helper needs to review what has been said and assess the reason for the silence.

4. Look like you are listening.

Different counseling approaches put varying degrees of emphasis on body language and the physical aspects of the counseling environment. How we sit, where we sit, our posture, and our eye contact are all topics for discussion and evaluation. The most important takeaway from those discussions is to look like we are paying attention and to show that we are listening by our physical and verbal responses to what the client has said. We look at the client, but don't stare. We face our client squarely, but we don't sit or stand so rigidly that we are uncomfortable. We make sure our facial expression is appropriate for the content of the client's statements and feelings. For example, we would not smile while a client is talking about being assaulted and robbed.

5. Listen to more than just the words being said.

- Listen to what is *not* being said. Are some topics avoided? Is the client telling only one side of the story or a slanted version of events? What is missing?
- Listen to facial expressions and body

language. Does the client's facial expression match the emotion of what is being said? Do facial expression and body language match? Does the client's body language change as the topic changes?
- Listen for themes, beliefs, and values of our client. Is there consistency between the client's stated values and actions? What are his or her core beliefs? What does our client believe about himself or herself? What does our client believe about people, in general?
- Listen for how our client has reacted and responded to challenges in the past. Has the client been resilient in the past? Does our client view himself or herself as a victim?
- Listen for the resources and helps in the client's life. Does our client have a support system? Does our client have friends and family who are consistently involved in his or her life? Does the client belong to any groups (church, civic organizations, special interest groups)?

Really listening involves so much more than just comprehending the words being said; it involves understanding the context. It is this understanding that leads to a productive collaborative relationship between a client and the helper. A relationship of this quality will make it possible for the helper to be a catalyst for change in the lives of others; not by telling them what to do, but by listening effectively to help them discover for themselves a preferred path.

OBSTACLES TO EFFECTIVE LISTENING

In addition to enhancing our knowledge of and skill at listening, it is also wise to identify and remove attitudes and practices that hinder effective listening. There are several levels of obstacles.

Effective listening is hard work that demands strong attention. Thus, we turn off the television and silence our devices. When careful listening is essential, we choose an environment that is safe and non-distracting. We stack the deck in favor of effective hearing.

Fatigue can be a major enemy of effective listening. High-level people-helping is emotionally draining. Thus, whenever we can, we avoid marathon counseling sessions. For most of us, it is quite challenging to listen at the highest level for more than about one hour. There are exceptions, but multiple shorter sessions are overwhelmingly the best choice.

Assumptions are a major deterrent to effective listening. Assumptions are unavoidable—and not necessarily bad. Think of them as hypotheses that move us toward understanding. That will work as long as we maintain humility as helpers. We hypothesize and listen in order to test our understanding. As we gain new insight, we revise and improve each hypothesis. Some, we discard as errant. Because we are working with and for God, truth remains paramount. We treat each person as unique and important. We refuse to give in to illusion or falsehood. We refuse to move to autopilot, having assumed that we already know this story because we've heard it all before. If we're not dealing with reality and the specific situation before us, we're in no position to help.

May we offer technique suggestion? It has been our practice to say to people whom we're trying to help, "I really want to listen well and understand where you're coming from. If you ever think that I'm not understanding, you're probably right. If that happens, look me in the eye and say, 'I don't think you are following me. Here's what I need you to know.'"

This technique acknowledges human limitations and models humility. It empowers the person we're helping to help us help them. It's also a form of insurance, offering something of a safety net as we serve.

Hands down, the most dangerous reason for poor listening is lack of love for the person we're trying to help. Caring demands listening; consistent, life-changing listening skills will be developed and practiced only by those who choose to care. Love will always find a way (1 Cor 13:7–8a). Love of God motivates us to give our best in helping others—including listening with skill and heart (Col 3:23–24). Love moves us to do our best and to keep asking God to make our best better (1 Thess 4:9–10).

CONCLUSION

Most of us have experienced the humbling joy of being listened to in love. We knew we were being honored and respected. We knew something wonderful was happening. We knew that we were experiencing the grace of God. And we know that God gives us the ability to show that same grace to others (1 Pet 4:10).

ENDNOTES

1. Mark W. Baker, *Jesus, The Greatest Therapist Who Ever Lived*, (New York: HarperOne, 2007).
2. Scott T. Meier and Susan R. Davis, *The Elements of Counseling*, 6th ed., (Thomson Brooks/Cole, 2008).
3. Donald Rumsfeld, U.S. Department of Defense news briefing, (February 12, 2002).
4. Gerard Egan and Robert Reese, *The Skilled Helper: A Problem-Management & Opportunity-Development Approach to Helping*, (Boston: Cengage, 2019).
5. Mark W. Baker, *Jesus, The Greatest Therapist Who Ever Lived*, (New York: HarperOne, 2007).

CHAPTER 6
THE BASICS OF EMPATHY

We hope you don't view empathy as "one of those strange humanistic counseling words." We don't. We don't think of empathy as a tool or technique. For us, it's foundational to any helping relationship. More than that, it's foundational to following Jesus. As we think of counseling for church leaders, we view empathy as a sub-category of godly love. "Empathy" is not a biblical word, but it's a biblical concept, principle, mandate, goal, and treasure.

THE COMPASSION OF JESUS

We see a hint of empathy in Jesus's submission to his parents (Luke 2:41–52). Even at the age of twelve, Jesus was blessed with amazing understanding and answers. He was more aware than even His parents of His unique role in His Father's business. Yet He chose to be submissive to them. He chose to show respect, connection, and appreciation. On the most practical of levels, He chose to show love.

We see a hint of empathy in Jesus's kind answer to His cousin John in Matthew 3:14. There's no command and no rebuke, more a polite request: "Let it be so, for this is fitting to fulfill all righteousness."

We see successive expressions of empathy and compassion from Jesus in Matthew 8. Rather than following the norm and emphasizing His physical safety, "Jesus stretched out His hand and touched him, saying, 'I will. Be clean!' And immediately his leprosy was cleansed." As Jesus's next miracle makes clear, the touch was not essential to the healing. The touch had a different purpose and a different meaning. We think it no reach to say that Jesus's touch was love, compassion, affirmation of their common humanity, and empathy. It was Jesus's way of saying, "I identify with you. I share in your pain and isolation. I affirm your worth before God. As God the Father loves you, so do I."

Following this physical expression of empathy comes a more thought-provoking expression. A centurion humbly requests healing for his suffering servant. Jesus responds, "I will come and heal him" (Matt 8:7). We know the story. The centurion affirms his faith that Jesus need not come under his unworthy roof: "Only say the word, and my servant will be healed." Why was Jesus so willing to help this Roman soldier? Surely, the soldier's faith was a major factor, but Jesus stood willing to go and heal even before the man's faith was fully expressed. Why? We suggest empathy for a fellow leader who cared about those in his service. Jesus could put Himself in the centurion's shoes, feel his pain, and share his burden.

Empathy is strongly implied in Matthew 8:16–17. It wasn't just that Jesus healed all comers. The prophecy that Matthew recognized as being fulfilled states, "He took our illnesses and bore our diseases" (Isa 53:5). Some translations begin that quotation with double emphasis, "He Himself took ..." (NKJV). Again, we see empathy in action.

We see empathy in the Bible's shortest verse, "Jesus wept" (John 11:35). His tears came after seeing the grief of Mary and those who accompanied her. We see empathy in Jesus's compassion for the multitudes who were "like sheep without a shepherd" (Matt 9:36). Jesus was repeatedly moved with compassion for the hurting and lost (Matt 14:14, 15:53, 20:34, 23:37).

THE COMPASSION OF GOD

While clearly demonstrated in the life of Jesus Christ, God's identification with and love for His people is seen in the Old Testament as well. It doesn't require much emotional imagination to feel God's heart pained over Cain's struggle with sin in Genesis 4:3–7. God, who cannot be tempted by evil (Jas 1:13, Heb 4:15), reached out to Cain with heartfelt warning and encouragement.

We see God's empathy and compassion in His dealings with Hagar and Ishmael (Gen 16:6–14, 21:14–21). Notice the Bible's emphasis on God's saving action after "God heard the voice of the boy." God heard, understood, connected, and cared.

Is empathy (understanding, connecting, and caring) implied in God's call of Moses to deliver His people from oppression? "I have surely seen the affliction of My people who are in Egypt and have heard their cry because of their taskmasters. I know their sufferings." (Exod 3:7). We assert that "know" speaks of more than knowing the facts; it speaks of God's personal concern and heart-connection. This thinking is strongly influenced by the words of Jesus to Saul in Acts 9:4 as well as the words of Jesus in Matthew 25:34–40.

Time and again, we see God's heartfelt concern through the Old Testament. Consider Daniel's faithful anguish in Daniel 9. Daniel read "the books" and knew that the end of the seventy-year captivity was near. He took his concern to God "by prayer and pleas for mercy with fasting and sackcloth and ashes" (Dan 7:3). Daniel's faith and confession so moved God that the Lord dispatched the angel Gabriel to offer comfort and reassurance (Dan 7:20ff). God owed no explanation. Reassuring Daniel was in no way essential to God's upcoming actions. God confirmed His word to Daniel out of love for his servant and respect for that servant's faithful heart.

It would be difficult to miss the pain in Isaiah's heart as he called his people back to God (Isa 1:1–20). While the condemnation of sin is justly stout, the pain of God and his prophet as they feel for and with the erring people are also evident. Lamentations 1 stands among the Bible's clearest descriptions of God's empathy with those who reject Him. He can neither approve nor excuse their rebellious choice, but still His heart goes out to them. He feels their pain.

THE BIBLICAL CALL TO COMPASSION

Calls to love, compassion, and understanding fill the pages of Scripture. "Let love be genuine" (Rom 12:9). "Rejoice with those who rejoice, weep with those who weep" (Rom 12:15). "Love bears all things, believes all things, hopes all things, endures all things" (1 Cor 13:7). "Be kind to one another, tenderhearted." (Eph 4:32). "Let each of you look not only to his own interests, but also to the interests of others" (Phil 2:4). "And above all these put on love, which binds everything together in perfect harmony (Col 3:14). "For this is the message that we have heard from the beginning, that we should love one another" (1 John 3:11). "We know that we have passed from death into life, because we love the brethren" (1 John 3:14). "Beloved, let us love one another, for love is from God, and whoever loves has been born of God and knows God. Anyone who does not love, does not know God, for God is love" (1 John 4:7–8).

Our assertion is that empathy—seeking to care, know, understand, and "feel with" others—is an aspect of love as defined and described in Scripture. The capacity for empathy is part of being made in the image of God (Gen 2:26–27). The choice to practice empathy is an essential part of imitating Christ.

BENEFITS OF EMPATHY

We know the truism: People don't care how much you know until they know how much you care. Like all proverbs, there are exceptions. Like all beneficial proverbs, the statement holds much truth.

When people know that we care, they tend to give us opportunities to help. Most of us avoid people who have no regard for us; it's human nature to do so. Showing empathy opens doors to greater service as Christian leaders.

When people believe that we care, they tend to listen more effectively. This is more than just paying more careful attention. When people believe we care, they listen with their hearts. They add what they know to what we're saying. They look for ways to understand rather than ways to discount and disagree. It's not that they turn off their critical thinking. They ask the crucial question: "Is what I'm hearing biblical, consistent, in keeping with reality, in accord with what godly people do?" Even as they ask, they practice critical thinking with kindness and compassion.

Even when we make mistakes when trying to help others, empathy blesses all parties. When we discover our errors, we'll accept responsibility for our mistakes, sincerely apologize, and make appropriate amends. Caring for and connecting with those we're helping will promote and empower such repentance. On the flip side, knowing that we care will make it both easier for forgiveness to happen—and more likely to happen without loss of trust or relationship.

Empathy makes us humble helpers. Empathy keeps us from imitating the Pharisee of Luke 18:11: "God, I thank You that I am not like other men." As we help others, empathy helps us avoid the traps of thinking too highly of or overestimating ourselves (Rom 12:3, 1 Cor 10:12). Empathy keeps us from imitating the priest and the Levite from Luke 10:25ff. Empathy won't allow us to do nothing when love demands action.

Empathy, as an aspect of love, also intersects 1 Corinthians 13:4–7. It tilts us toward patience and kindness. Empathy stands in the way of envy, arrogance, and selfishness. It promotes optimism, perseverance and creativity. Love will find a way.

Finally, a commitment to grow in empathy is a commitment to grow. 2 Peter 1 strongly supports such growth as it urges us to add both brotherly affection and love. While that passage and 1 Thessalonians 4:9–10 address far more than just empathy, caring for and connecting with those we help are surely included.

COSTS OF EMPATHY

Conveying empathy is an art that doesn't come naturally to everyone. It is an art that can be learned, but learning requires practice, commitment, and humility. If empathy is not wisely conveyed, it will be perceived as insincere, as a manipulative technique. Or it will be perceived as condescension. "Poor little dumb you. You don't know how to manage your pain or your life." Learning to convey empathy in a helpful manner requires an impressive tolerance for pain on the part of the learner. We won't always get it right. Some of our errors will be both harmful and embarrassing.

Empathy comes at considerable emotional cost. It's the polar opposite of the cynical proverb: "Sincerity is THE thing. If you can fake that, you've got it made." Rather, empathy is Galatians 6:2 in action: "Bear one another's burdens and so fulfill the law of Christ." It's Romans 12:15, "Rejoice with those who rejoice, weep with those who weep." It's powerfully described in Paul's pain list of 2 Corinthians 11:28–29: "And, apart from other things, there is the daily pressure on me of my anxiety for all the churches. Who is weak, and I am not weak? Who is made to fall, and I am not indignant?" And Paul chose these words as the apex of his list of the burdens that he bore for the sake of Christ (2 Cor 11:23ff). To be blunt, caring deeply for others isn't always suffering, but it is always a psychological and a spiritual burden.

Empathy comes at considerable personal cost. If we choose to help hurting people, there will be times when we care more about them than they care about themselves. There also will be times when we care about them more wisely and spiritually than they care about themselves. In such times, helpers bear an extra set of burdens. Are our efforts appreciated? Are they sufficiently appreciated to justify our continued efforts? Is it right/wise/proper for us as helpers to care more than the people we're trying to help? Is this imbalanced condition temporary? Does it have a Godward resolution? At the end of the sequence, will their gain be worth our pain? The answers to such questions are seldom clear and certain.

OBJECTIONS TO EMPATHY

Some object to a call to empathy on the basis of faith and philosophy. "Empathy isn't a biblical word. It's a counseling concept flowing from a secular and humanistic mindset." For some people helpers, this will be true.

But we believe we have made a biblical case for God-honoring, Christ-following, biblically-guided empathy. No concept is inherently wrong just because it has been articulated and promoted from a humanistic perspective.

Some raise a different philosophical objection to the importance of empathy within a Christian counseling context. "We deal in facts, not feelings. We deal in the truth of God that frees, saves, and sanctifies (John 8:32, 17:17; 2 Thess 2:10; 1 Tim 2:4). We don't have time to be distracted by feelings. Truth has nothing to do with empathy." We reject this thinking as cold and unbiblical.

We love truth and appreciate Jesus as "the way, the truth, and the life" (John 14:6). Even as the embodiment of truth, Jesus's personal love and tenderness pervade the gospels. To present feelings as the opposite or the enemy of facts is a false dichotomy denied by Scripture. While emotionalism is extreme and, therefore, dangerous, God created us as emotional beings. While love is not merely an emotion, biblical love includes vital emotional components.

There is at least one additional major objection to empathy within counseling for church leaders: the assertion that empathy condones error, that empathy is, by definition, soft on sin. "If I listen with care and concern to people whose challenges obviously flow from sinful behavior, they will think that I excuse, approve, or support their sin." We can't deny that people could make this unwarranted assumption. We strongly deny that this assumption has any validity or support from Scripture.

No teaching or practice can be considered invalid or unbiblical just because it can be misunderstood. Rather, we teach and practice God's truth with all due diligence and care. God didn't condone the sins of Adam and Eve by listening to them and caring for them (Gen 3). He demonstrated obvious concern for Cain in Genesis 4, but in no sense excused Cain's sin. Jesus extended great heart toward the woman caught in adultery, even refusing to condemn her to death. Still, His parting words were, "Neither do I condemn you, go, and sin no more" (John 8:11). Jesus demonstrated empathy even for those who committed history's greatest atrocity (Luke 23:34). Yet, in no sense was He condoning their sin of murder (Acts 2:22–23, 36–39).

HOW IS EMPATHY DEMONSTRATED?

On the most modest level, empathy is demonstrated by presence in time of need. There's notable power in just showing up and investing our time. The highlight of the empathy of Job's friends was in showing up, grieving with him, and sitting in silence (Job 2:11–13). It's what Jesus asked His disciples to do on the night of the betrayal (Matt 26:36–38). Sometimes, people's primary need is to be "watched with," to have us stand with them so that they know they're not alone.

Heartfelt listening demonstrates empathy. Some have described this as listening with "heart, soul, strength, and mind" (Luke 10:27). In our culture, it means silencing the cellphone and other devices. It means refusing to be distracted. It means doing our best to align our hearts with the person we want to help. We look awake and concerned with culturally appropriate eye contact and posture. They can see our concern in our faces. Our body language (movements or lack thereof) tells them that we hear, we care, and we want to understand. As noted above, our silence can speak volumes.

When the time comes to speak, our choice of words either reflects or denies true empathy. We avoid cliché and truism: "I know just how you feel." "This too shall pass." "You'll feel better soon." "Time heals all wounds." We avoid false comfort: "Everything will be okay." "We'll look back at this one day and laugh." We avoid minimization: "This isn't nearly as big a deal as it seems." "Things could be worse." We avoid judgment of feelings: "You shouldn't cry." "You shouldn't yell." "You shouldn't be angry." We're careful about our judgement of actions: "You shouldn't have done that." "You shouldn't have said that." "That was really dumb." Empathy demands that we express truth without insult, that we express both truth and love.

In demonstrating empathy, some words of comfort—if heartfelt and true—are almost always appropriate: "I love you." "God loves you." "We are here for you." "We're with you." "You're not in this alone."

On another level, hurting people need affirmation that we hear and understand them. There's power in restating what you have just been told. We don't go robotic. We don't overdo. We don't dramatize. Rather, we reassure in the spirit of Matthew 7:12 and Philippians 2:3–4. We do our best to treat people like we'd want to be treated in the same situation.

A caveat is in order for the last statement. We treat people like we'd want to be treated while allowing for individual uniqueness. Some of us need few words;

empathy, comfort, and support are primarily nonverbal. "Don't tell me that you care; show me. Actions speak far louder than words." Others need and value our words. If we don't say it, it isn't real. If we don't say it, then we don't care. The better we know the people we're helping, the better we can tailor and individualize our empathetic expression. That's a major advantage for church leaders. We tend to know our church family.

In fairness, knowing our church family is both a benefit and a potential trap. The benefit is obvious. The trap lies in the level of expectation. From a biblical perspective, brethren expect us to care (John 13:34-35, 1 Pet 1:22 and 3:17). Knowing the people we're helping lets us connect with them more quickly and at a more personal level. At the same time, it raises their expectations regarding both our ability and our responsibility to connect and serve with love.

Bottom line: People won't give us much chance to help them unless they believe that we care. Most people won't believe that we care unless we show them. Empathy is a crucial aspect of showing our love.

CHAPTER 7
THE BASICS OF EMOTION

One of the most complex aspects of helping others is understanding the nature, purposes, and complexity of human emotion. Positively, emotions motivate and energize. They add spice and variety to life. They protect us from danger. They endear us to people who bless our lives. Positively, the Bible ascribes many emotions to God, particularly compassion (Exod 22:27, Deut 32:36, 2 Kgs 13:24, Ps 103:13 & 135:14, Isa 55:7). We love the gospels' emphasis on the compassion of Jesus (Matt 9:36, 14:14, 15:32; Luke 7:13). Fairness demands that we also note God's anger (Num 11:1, 10, 33). Mark 3:5 documents the anger of Jesus as He saw people's hardness of heart.

Our emotional capacity is one of the ways we are made in the image of God (Gen 3:26–27). Despite our occasional wish that we could "turn them off," emotions are a fundamental element of our common humanity. Emotions are powerful, but not evil.

Of course God's emotions are always in perfect balance and control (Exod 34:6, Num 14:18). In this sin-damaged world, the same cannot be said of us. One way of looking at human function is that we all possess the ability to think, act, and feel. At our best, we think and act biblically. We think and act in light of God's existence, God's revelation, God's love for us, our love for God, and God's ultimate judgment. As a broad rule, good feelings follow good actions. Bad actions can originate from bad—undisciplined, ungodly—thinking (Gen 6:5, Ps 36:4, Mic 2:1). They can also flow from letting our emotions rule our thinking—think of Joseph's brothers' actions that flowed from their envy, jealousy, and hatred (Gen 37). We acknowledge that in the ebb and flow of daily life, we often don't parse our motivations by category. We also acknowledge that the interplay of thought, action, and emotion is more complicated than we can grasp.

As shown by Joseph's brothers, emotions can also motivate and energize on sinful and destructive levels. There had to be an emotional component to Mrs. Potiphar's overtures toward Joseph (Gen 39). In jealousy and rage, Saul tried to kill his loyal servant David (1 Sam 18). Old anger and bitterness led Shimei to curse King David (2 Sam 16). Emotional intensity is obvious in those who eventually murdered Jesus (Matt 9:3 & 34, 12:14 & 24, 15:1–2 & 12, 21:12–16 & 45–46, 23:15, 26:3–4 & 57–68, and 27:20–25). Stephen's own countrymen murdered him in a fit of rage (Acts 7). Powerful emotion is obvious in Paul's critics (Acts 13:45, 14:1–7, 17:5–9, 21:26–36, and 22:22–24).

A CAVEAT

There is room for debate regarding our understanding of terms that speak of emotion, action, and thinking. For example, the Bible uses the word "love" to speak of Amnon's illicit feelings for Tamar (2 Sam 13:1 & 15). While inspired of God, Scripture is a real-world book that communicates on a real-world level. But we know that Amnon's feelings and actions were the very opposite of Matthew 22:34–40; John 3:16, 13:34-35, & 15:15; and 1 Corinthians 13.

CATEGORIES OF EMOTION

Humans have the capacity to feel mad, glad, sad, scared, and bored. Many have an expanded view of the range of emotion expressed in these five words. As you work to help others, we recommend never quibbling over the words that hurting people use to describe their emotions. For example, if you say to a hurting person, "You certainly seem angry today," and he responds, "I'm not angry, I'm furious," choose to use his word and let him express his feelings his way. Let him describe the level of intensity. If he has mislabeled his feelings, that will come to light in due time. If his feelings are more intense than they should be, you will help guide him to self-discovery and moderation. Precision in wording is not nearly as important as building rapport, inviting thought, and showing love.

EMOTION 101

Researchers suggest three primary components of emotion.[1] We present this not for the sake of technical knowledge, but because it has value in helping people understand and deal with their emotional challenges.

Initially comes emotional arousal. Our minds become aware of and our bodies respond to an emotion. The physical response may come before the awareness. For example, blood pressure rises and heart rate increases. We may go into fight or flight mode.

Next comes emotional expression. We act in response to our emotional awareness. The action can be verbal, non-verbal, or a combination.

Emotional experience is the third component. We feel what we feel about both the initial emotion and our response to it.

There is a secondary component of emotion— emotional reflection. We have the ability to evaluate each of the primary components listed above.

How can this knowledge help us help others? It is healthy to recognize and accurately identify our own emotions. The earlier we do this, the more options we have. If we realize our heart rate is increasing, we may choose to take a deep breath and tell ourselves to stay calm. This is appropriate and beneficial when there is no immediate physical danger. Questions such as the ones that follow can help monitor emotional processes:

- Is this new to me, or have I been here before?
- If I've been here before, what came next?

- Was what came next helpful or harmful? If it wasn't optimal, what choices might I have?

We can intervene even more in the area of emotional expression. We recommend teaching people to ask themselves the following questions:

- Am I thinking about what I'm going to do next, or am I in danger of going on autopilot? Thinking is highly recommended.
- In what ways is this situation like and unlike similar previous situations? What differences do I need to consider? Am I dealing with these feelings fairly in the current context, or am I letting old pain overly influence me?
- What are my behavioral options? What can I choose to do next? In some cases, the best option is to walk away—think of a potential confrontation with a stranger. Sometimes the best option is to explain your perspective. A classic option, especially when strong negative emotions are sparked in a family setting, is to ask, "I know we need to talk about this, but could I have a few minutes to think (or pray) first?" Almost never is the best option to catastrophize and escalate the situation. Almost never is the best option to hit, throw, or break something.

Many people do not know that there are decision points in the process of emotional expression. Many assume a "direct drive" relationship between emotion and action. In schoolyard terms, "Ralph, why did you hit Johnny?" "He hit me, so I hit him back." Reality is more complex. It would bless Ralph to be taught that he had the ability to process the situation and to weigh his options. Pertinent questions include

- Did Johnny mean to hit me, or could it have been an accident?
- Did I do something to provoke the hit? If so, might I want to change my behavior?
- Was the "hit" an attack or a playful gesture?
- Has Johnny hit me before? Is this part of an ongoing pattern of abuse?
- Will Johnny beat me to a pulp if I hit him back?
- What if I yell or seek help instead of hitting back? What are the social costs—I don't want to be labeled a rat or a coward.
- What if I choose to ignore him? Will Johnny see that as strength and leave me alone, or will he perceive weakness and escalate the attack?

Please elevate our schoolyard example to applicable adult settings. Church members don't normally hit with fists; more often they use words. Still the basic questions apply. There's strong negative emotion over feeling attacked. Are there options that honor Matthew 5:9 and 43–48? What of Romans 12:18–21? In your efforts to help, invite biblical thinking and creativity in the application of godly principles.

In terms of both emotional experience and emotional reflection, there is great benefit in reminding people that we have the ability to shape our memories. This capacity is imperfect and limited, but also powerful. We can, as it were, file a negative emotional experience as relationship-destroying and life-defining. On the other hand, we can—with God's help—file it as one painful and undesirable episode that will not be allowed to define who we are or whom we love.

Particularly in the area emotional reflection, additional questions include

- In what ways, if any, did I contribute to this situation? How might I have prevented or mitigated the conflict?
- What do my feelings about this event say about my character? Am I being who and what God wants me to be? If not, what's my plan for improvement?
- Did I control my feelings or did my feelings control me?
- Can I identify a default position when there are strong negative emotions? If so, is my default position healthy? If not, how can I work to change it?

Emotion is energy. For good or bad, feelings animate life. We are "wired" for emotion from birth, but our "wiring" isn't the whole story. From our earliest years, we learn to manage our emotions. In healthy families we learn self-control, turn-taking, teamwork, and forgiveness. Unhealthy families often teach selfishness, bullying, and manipulation. As church leaders, it's important that we NOT assume that everyone had the same godly examples and instruction that we enjoyed. Some people don't manage their emotions because they don't know that they can—or they don't know how. Our work with these members will focus on basic education.

Admittedly, some know that they can control their emotions and even have the skills to do so. But they don't choose to use those skills. Our work with them will focus on welcoming the new heart and new mind that come with the new birth.

Even those who possess both knowledge and skills will possess them in varying degrees. Our work sometimes involves improving and expanding those attributes.

Emotions are real. Learning to recognize and own our emotions is an essential part of maturing. Unfortunately, society often teaches denial of emotion: "Big boys don't cry." "Real men don't say, 'I love you.'" Emotional shutdown is a classic relationship killer. It just as effectively kills joy. Emotional denial is anti-truth and anti-trust. It leaves us in a poor position to build loving families and lasting friendships. We're not speaking against promoting socially appropriate behaviors, but we oppose promoting strength and stability at the expense of emotional health.

As implied above, emotional maturity is a life-long process. We don't expect the same level of emotional awareness and mature expression from a preschooler and an octogenarian. Twin dangers exist. We could give way to unfair expectations that children become mini-adults, holding them to unrealistic standards. Oppositely, we could tolerate childishness in adults—including ourselves. Life-long growth toward Jesus is the goal (Luke 2:52, Eph 4:11–15).[2]

Emotions are scary. Most of us are uncomfortable in the presence of raw negative emotion. We find it challenging to be in the presence of deep pain or hot anger. We struggle in the presence of weeping. These realities are a major reason that some avoid helping those who are hurting. Caring church leaders cannot choose that option.

We offer the following suggestions for finding the strength to deal with raw emotion. Realize that you are under no obligation to stop those emotions. It is not within your power to stop them, and it could be counterproductive if you did.

Realize that dramatic emotional expression can be an aspect of healthy venting. We've heard wise people speak of "crying out the hurt" or "yelling out the pain." Giving people a safe space in which to express their pain is godly work. The rule of thumb is—short of absurd extremes or venting that is destructive of others—"let happen what happens." It is reasonable to ask, "How do I do that? How do I stay calm, thoughtful, and engaged in the presence of emotional turmoil?" Experience helps. Self-talk can help. "It's okay to feel uncomfortable. This is not about me or my comfort. Even extreme discomfort isn't fatal. I'm doing what God would have me do. This is not permanent. They need me."

To be blunt, listening to people express strong negative emotion is no one's favorite part of helping others.

Some even deny that such listening is actually helpful. We think it is. Even if we are wrong on that point, it is a precursor to helping.

From a developmental perspective, our personal goal is to possess the emotional competence that lets us help others. Our goal when helping others is to assist them in reaching emotional competence. Saarni offers a list of key skills for emotional competence.[3] It begins with awareness of our own emotions. From that foundation, we gain the ability to discern and understand the emotions of others. We will never be flawless or complete in this understanding. Thus, we use the phrase "emotional competence" rather than "emotional mastery" or "emotional perfection."

From the ability to discern and understand—to some positive degree—the emotions of others, we move to the ability to use the vocabulary of emotion. On the simplest level, ask a husband in marriage counseling, "How do you feel about your wife?" With stunning frequency, he will answer, "I'm faithful to her. I work hard. I come home very night. I take care of the yard." He will list loving actions, but seldom will include a single word about how he feels, about emotion. One of our jobs in helping people is to expand their vocabulary. Initially, we may mention a feeling that they can't quite name. Eventually, we help them learn to speak in the language of both head and heart.

EMOTIONAL COMPETENCE

We highly value the concept of emotional competence. It provides a framework for using both our understanding of emotion and our emotions themselves to help others. Emotional competence must include the practice of empathy—in fact, it may be that there can be no practice of empathy without emotional competence.[4] In order to help, we must be able to show that we care and that we want to understand.

Emotional competence includes the ability to differentiate feelings (emotional experience) from actions (external expression in response to our emotions). As discussed above, it is crucial to know that an emotion—no matter how strong—does not directly cause an action. We choose our actions based on how we process our emotions.

Emotional competence includes the ability to cope with major challenges. We fix what we can fix; we endure what we can't fix; and we choose to endure with dignity, faith, and love. Otherwise, we crumble or become bitter. Crumbling leaves us victims and invites additional pain. Bitterness removes joy and taints every facet of life.

Emotional competence includes awareness of emotional communication within relationships. Think of Willard Harley's classic *His Needs, Her Needs*.[5] Harley describes the love bank within each person's heart. If the account balance is positive, the relationship thrives. If it goes red, trouble is imminent. The metaphor of the love bank sets up excellent recommendations. Chief among them is the reminder that what I consider (or intend) to be a deposit into my spouse's love bank may not be. If I clumsily mismatch and fail to meet either needs or expectations, the attempted deposit can be perceived as a withdrawal. When making deposits, it's not what I think or prefer. The key question is, "Does my spouse value this? Does it speak to his/her heart?" Lack of awareness of emotional communication within relationships—whether marriage or otherwise—leads to countless failed deposit attempts.

Another example is Gary Chapman's *The Five Languages of Love*.[6] Even if there are more than five languages of love, Chapman's key point is undeniable. Unless we practice emotional competence by "speaking" a love language that those we love can understand, we're failing to express and build love. The devil will tempt us to assert, "The people I deal with just need to expand their vocabulary. They need to step up and listen my way." Of course, Matthew 7:12 and Philippians 2:3–4 do not support such thinking. And that approach never works.

Finally, emotional competence includes the ability to choose, manage, and direct our emotions in a moral and loving way. For the consummate example, we think of Hebrews 12:2, "Looking to Jesus, the founder and perfecter of our faith, who for the joy that was set before him endured the cross, despising the shame, and is seated at the right hand of the throne of God." Read that verse in light of the agony expressed in Matthew 26:36–46, where Jesus was "sorrowful and troubled" and "very sorrowful, even to death." He chose, managed, and directed His emotions in a world-changing moral and loving manner.

For a lesser, but still stunning example, think of the apostle Paul. Philippians, the joy book of the New Testament (Phil 4:4), was written by Paul from prison. He speaks of God's overruling grace even when some worked to harm him (Phil 1:15–18). Even from prison, he includes the words, "I have received full payment, and more." (Phil 4:18a). Philippians 4:11–13 speaks directly to Paul's grace-given ability to choose, manage, and direct both his emotions and his attitude. It's beautiful teaching on the intersection of spiritual and emotional health.

ENDNOTES

[1.] The bulk of the content in this section flows from two seminal works. Carolyn Saarni, *The Development of Emotional Competence* (New York: Guilford Press, 1999). Eileen Kenney-Moore and Jeannie C. Watson, *Expressing Emotion: Myths, Realities, and Therapeutic Strategies* (New York: Guilford Press, 1999). Additional foundational material is available from James J. Gross, ed., *Handbook of Emotional Regulation* (New York: Guilford Press, 2014), and Lisa F. Barrett, Michael Lewis, and Jeanne H. M. Haviland-Jones, eds., *Handbook of Emotions* (New York: Guilford Press 2016). A more recent work from a Christian perspective is J. Alasdair Groves and Winston T. Smith, *Untangling Emotions* (Wheaton, IL: Crossway, 2019).
[2.] For a curriculum suggestion for teaching about emotional maturity, see chapter 20, "The Power of Prevention."
[3.] Saarni, *The Development of Emotional Competence*.
[4.] See chapter 6, "The Basics of Empathy."
[5.] Willard F. Harley, Jr., *His Needs, Her Needs: Building an*

Affair-Proof Marriage, Fifteenth Anniversary ed., (Grand Rapids: Fleming H. Revell, 2001).

6. Gary Chapman, *The Five Languages of Love: How to Express Heartfelt Commitment to Your Mate* (Chicago: Northfield Publishers, 1992).

CHAPTER 8

TRAPS TO AVOID

Counseling includes working with hurting people during painful and challenging times. When the process goes well, it's both rewarding and exhausting. When it doesn't, it's core-of-the-soul challenging. Counseling often involves personal and family secrets. Frequently, it's highly emotive. While our goal is to help, Satan's goal is to use the counseling process to divide, discourage, and destroy. And He knows just the traps to set.

TRAPS OF OVERESTIMATION

I must help everyone who asks. This trap comes in different forms. Satan would have us focus on the word "I." "I, uniquely and individually, must provide the counseling help that this person needs." Admittedly, there are situations that seem to match our skills and experience. God puts us in the right place at the right time to serve with particular effectiveness. We don't want to create imaginary traps. Far more often, we will be part of a team of helpers. And we do not need to lead every helping team. We are not qualified to lead every team. It's a blessing to let others lead and for us to model "followship."

Given the demands of life and the reality of only 24 hours in each day, it may be impossible for us to personally and directly help everyone who asks. Counseling eats energy. It's not selfish to set boundaries. Running life past the red line is not sustainable. Something will break or blow up. Even before that happens, the quality of our helping will diminish. Sometimes the best way to help people who ask is to help them find the best resource. We won't always be the best option.

Nothing is beyond my reach. The enhanced version of this trap may even quote scripture: "I can do all things through him who strengthens me" (Phil 4:13). "There's no need, issue, person, or problem that I can't address effectively." In context, "do" in Philippians 4:13 is best understood as "endure" or "face" or "overcome." In light of Romans 12:3, it cannot be an assertion of absolute confidence in the boundless nature of our personal talents. Humility demands that we recognize our limitations and avoid overestimating our ability to help. The time-honored counseling mantra is "It's unethical to counsel beyond your competency."

I can run on overload. Some call this the Superman Complex. "No matter my level of overload and exhaustion, I must soldier on. If I don't meet these needs, nobody will. Scaling back or taking a break is weakness and lack of faith." Humans can't run on continual overload. Judgment diminishes, attention levels decrease, and higher-order skills decline.[1] Even Jesus took needed breaks from the pressures of ministry (Mark 1:35 & 6:31).

I fully understand this person and this situation. The counseling phrase "the presenting problem" offers major help here. The presenting problem is a person's stated reason for coming to see the counselor. Often, it is **a** reason rather than **the** reason. The hurting person may not yet be able to state the reason. He may need to establish additional trust before stating the reason. She may be in denial—hiding the primary need even from herself.

Wise counselors listen and formulate hypotheses. Wise counselors avoid assumptions. Wise counselors tweak or abandon initial hypotheses as they learn more. Especially within a church setting, we may know the person whom we're helping. We may know several generations of his family. Though usually helpful, such knowledge also carries a temptation. We can assume that we know the issues, needs, challenges, strengths, and personalities involved. And the devil, as it were, whispers in our ear, "No need to listen and learn. You've got this." What a trap!

I'm above the temptations that afflict others. The classic example in this category is assuming immunity from sexual temptation. Most church leaders are male, and the majority of church members are female. Loving attempts to help can be misperceived as sexual interest. A touch or a compliment can be perceived as an overture. And no one is above temptation (1 Cor 10:12).

We offer two STRONG recommendations. Always observe due propriety and practice environmental excellence. Do not make yourself an easy target for temptation. Don't meet where you should not meet. Put intelligent safeguards in place. Secondly, if you find yourself having any sexual thoughts about the hurting person you are helping, immediately find the person a new helper. Playing with temptation is like a mouse playing with a cat.

TRAPS OF UNDERESTIMATION

I have nothing to offer. In today's world, it seems that far more people overestimate rather than underestimate their talents. But within church settings, underestimation still thrives. We respect Romans 12:3 and Galatians 6:3, and we know the dangers of pride (Prov 16:18, 1 Pet 5:5–7). We must also respect Exodus 3 and 4. God did not accept Moses' excuse or his request to be exempted from service. The parable of the talents strongly implies that each servant had something with which to serve his master (Matt 25). Ephesians 4:11–16 powerfully teaches that every part of the body has something to contribute to unity, stability, and edification.[2] We dare not let the devil tell us what we can't do for God. Even worse would be our choosing to tell God He has failed to equip us to serve.

Counseling is not my thing. As you know, this book takes an expansive view of counseling as virtually any form of people-helping that involves listening and loving. We do not assert that everyone should become a therapist. Helping people by listening and loving is not optional for any Christian, especially those who lead. Think of Matthew 7:12, Romans 12:4–13, 1 Corinthians

12:4–31, and Galatians 6:1–10. No one is as utterly defeated as the person who chooses not to try.

This hurting person is doomed. Sometimes it's not a matter of the counselor underestimating himself. Sometimes we underestimate the Lord's ability to effect change. Though we'd never express it in those words, we can say to ourselves, "There's no reason to try to help this person. There's too much baggage. There's not enough capacity. There's just no reason to try." We never know enough to make such claims. We have no way to know what God will do if we plant and water faithfully. We have no way to know who will take their new heart and new mind and do great things for God. When he denied, we would never have seen Peter preaching on Pentecost. When he persecuted, we would never have seen Paul as a church planter. Our congregations are filled with people who have been utterly changed by the gospel.

TRAPS OF UNREALISTIC EXPECTATIONS

If my faith is strong enough, God will fix this. God will always do right, but on the detailed level, we almost never know specifically what God will do or how He will do it. We know that faith is essential (Hab 2:3, Rom 1:16, Heb 11:6). Daniel 3:16–18 offers us major help. To the best of our knowledge, Daniel's three friends had no assurance of physical deliverance from the furnace. They strongly asserted their faith: "Our God whom we serve is able to deliver us from the burning fiery furnace, and he will deliver us out of your hand, O king." At the same time, they acknowledged their limited knowledge of how or when—immediately or in the world to come—their deliverance would come.

The bottom line is clear; no matter how much confidence we have in God's power and goodness, we dare not promise more than God has said. God created and loves marriage, but divorces happen. God loves children, but children sometimes die. God loves His children, but houses burn, health crashes, and careers end tragically. The trap of speaking where God has not spoken is both tempting and horribly destructive.

I must fix this. Practically and philosophically, this is a terrible statement. Counselors do not fix people. We don't have that power. Even God, who has all power, does not "fix" people without their consent and cooperation. On top of that, some situations cannot be "fixed" because they involve multiple people, some of whom choose to persist in rebellion.

If I don't fully fix this, then I've failed; I've done no good at all. Satan loves the double-bind of the all or nothing trap. "Unless you totally resolve the situation and everyone leaves happy, you have failed as a counselor." Life is too complicated to believe such assertions. We highly recommend thinking holistically about helping people. As church leaders, we do what God allows us to do. But the person or people whom we are helping also have a role. The broader church community also plays a part.

On occasion God blesses our counseling efforts with obvious major success. We love those moments. They are both precious and rare. As a rule, the results of our counseling efforts are more measured and subtle. Sometimes, the outcome isn't relief or resolution; sometimes, it's finding the strength to endure and wait on the Lord. Sometimes it's learning to accept and function in a new and less desirable reality.

A word of warning: beware of counting counseling successes and failures. Appearances can deceive. Sessions that look and feel terrible can lead to positive breakthroughs. Sessions that seem stunningly productive can prove to be just smoke and mirrors. What do we do given this complexity and uncertainty? Choose to count faithful effort as success. Remember the power of "yet." "God has not yet delivered." "Your child hasn't repented yet." "Your heart is not at peace yet." The power of realistic biblical hope cannot be overstated.

There's a simple easy answer; my job is to find it. A secular proverb says, "For every complex problem, there's a solution that's easy, simple, and wrong." We appreciate both the humor and the wisdom. Easy answers seldom exist. Getting better is often hard work. The counseling rule of thumb is "it will take about as long to improve a situation as it took to create the situation." We love 1 Corinthians 10:13, but we realize that it does not promise an easy, quick, painless, or cost-free means of escape.

Everyone wants to get better. Not everyone seeks counseling in order to heal, bless, improve, or draw closer to God. Some come seeking vindication for their hatred or harmful actions. Some come seeking validation for their unbiblical thinking. Some come seeking absolution from a church leader—absolution without remorse or repentance. Admittedly, it's crushing to realize, "As counselor, I'm working harder at this than the people I'm trying to help." It's even worse to realize,

"I'm being played. To the best of my ability to know, they have no intention to change." All we know to do in such cases is to pray and to steadfastly refuse to join the game.

Christians always tell the truth. Counseling preys on the naive. While we must avoid cynicism, realism is essential. Nothing good comes of a lie. We love truth, seek truth, practice truth, and promote truth. When we realize that a person is being untruthful, we challenge them—fairly and lovingly. We work to help them see the value of truth and the relationship between truth and trust. To be blunt, some people are more skilled at deception than we are at detection. Still, truth is fierce. It does not tend to stay hidden. Part of effective counseling is refusing to ignore contradictions and inconsistencies. We want to help people come clean with themselves and with God.

CHARACTER TRAPS

Talking out of school. The word within counseling circles is confidentiality. Unless harm is being done to or planned against someone, we do not tell others what goes on in counseling. On the rare occasion when we learn that harm is being done or planned, the Golden Rule demands that we act to protect those who are in danger. Still, counseling is about building trust and working to help form a foundation of trust. Few actions destroy trust like making private information public. From a legal perspective, it can lead to court. From a spiritual perspective, the costs are even higher. Confidentiality flows from personal integrity. Those who breach confidentiality always get caught (Matt 12:36, 2 Cor 5:9–11).

Lack of tolerance for ambiguity. What the Bible condemns as wrong is wrong; what scripture identifies as right is right (Ps 119:105–112, John 8:37–38). While our trust in God's word is solid, we appreciate the challenge of applying biblical teachings across cultures and generations. Romans 14 acknowledges that challenge. Where the Bible speaks and specifies, we listen and obey. Where the Bible offers freedom to choose, we respect that freedom. It can be tempting for church leaders to think, "Life will be smoother if you just share my opinions." We have no right to impose our opinions on others. There's great blessing in loving, respectful, biblical flexibility.

A second trap regarding tolerance for ambiguity relates to the previous discussion of "I fully understand this person and this situation." As we help others, we continually acknowledge the limits of our understanding. We continually embrace increasing both the depth and breadth of our understanding. We don't know until we know, and even then we're wise to check behind ourselves.

STRATEGIC TRAPS

Chasing people. We love the fact that Jesus came to seek and save the lost (Luke 19:10). We love church leaders who are proactive in watching for the souls of others (Gal 6:1–5, Heb 13:17). When people we love obviously need counseling, there can be a temptation to pursue and pressure. If people feel pressured into counseling, the process seldom goes well. As urgent as spiritual matters are, we're blessed to tread lightly. We're blessed to invite and encourage rather than to pressure. It can be stunningly difficult to wait, but sometimes waiting gives the Lord time to work as it gives us time to pray and prepare.

Taking temporary control. Perhaps you have heard of the well-meaning, but misguided, church leader who said to a young couple, "I can save your marriage. If you will promise to do everything I say, I guarantee your marriage will not fail." We won't judge the motive, but the statement smacks of over-confidence. The "I language" is concerning.

On another level, there's great danger that the young couple might take him up on his offer. They might agree to let him run their lives for a time. That's a fearsome responsibility. None of us are that wise or that good. We want to teach, guide, support, and encourage. We don't want to control and assume responsibility at a level God has not approved.

Lone Rangerism. This trap relates closely to "I must help everyone who asks." It's "I—and I alone—must help everyone who asks." We're wise to remember Ecclesiastes 4:9-12. We're wise to remember that Jesus sent His disciples two by two and that the Holy Spirit called disciples for the first formal mission team. The secular proverb "We are smarter than me" also comes to mind. God has not called us to serve without support and teamwork.

What worked last time will work now. You know this trap if you've ever repeated a Bible class. Your plan can work beautifully in one setting but disappoint in another. It just doesn't click, and you may never know why. When it comes to tools and techniques of counseling, we recommend having a big toolbox. When recommending options to a person being helped, we recommend offering a menu of choices. Offering a menu removes the perception of giving orders. It's also psychologically sound. If we offer options and a choice is made, the people being helped feel empowered. They feel pulled to make their choice work. They often embrace their choice with a healthy sense of ownership.

What works for me will work for everyone. Your authors are book people. Reading has blessed us immeasurably. It's natural when we counsel to recommend bibliotherapy—to recommend that those we're helping read solid and helpful material. We think it will help them. With ever-increasing frequency, we'll recommend a book only to hear, "I'm not much of a reader." How do we respond? We make a different recommendation, one that fits the skills and personality of the person we're helping. There is no virtue in recommending solutions or activities that don't fit. Demanding that such activities be attempted never blesses.

Becoming an enabler. The literature of co-dependency is vast. Fundamentally, it warns against becoming part of the problem that you're trying to solve. Classic examples include bringing unhealthy food to a friend who's morbidly obese or covering up for an alcoholic family member so she escapes many consequences of her drinking.

An example of enabling more common to church leaders who counsel is allowing a person to rail against others without encouraging the practice of Matthew

5:21–26 and 18:15–20. Similarly, we could offer unwise support to a workaholic who is neglecting his family and regular worship of God (Prov 23:4–5 & 30:7–9, Luke 12:15). It is particularly tempting to enable people who share our unbiblical tendencies.

Disappointing endings. Ending a counseling relationship can present challenges. If things did not go well, some feel a need to assign blame. Others feel a need for excessive self-criticism. In the saddest of cases, hard words lead to hard feelings and broken relationships.

We offer three recommendations. End as positively as is possible. Stay honest, but leave bridges intact. Second, state the obvious. If true, say, "I know we didn't accomplish what we had hoped, but I want you to know that I appreciate your effort." If the last phrase isn't accurate, substitute "but I'll keep praying." Finally, reflect and assess. Why didn't things go better? What might I have done differently? What have I learned from this? The pain of disappointment is mitigated at least a bit if we learn from the experience.

Failing to trust the process. We hope you know that counseling is a process of learning to communicate, building trust, exploring options, and choosing to grow. That complicated and blessed process takes the time that it takes. There are no shortcuts; to rush it is to ruin it.

You may have excellent insight and see the final stages of the process weeks ahead of the people you are helping. If so, keep that to yourself. Don't violate the process of guided discovery. Don't rob those people of the opportunity for their "ah ha" moment. Let them have that moment, and they'll love you forever.

The process of counseling is almost always zigzag. There will be progress and setbacks; there are rabbit trails and foxholes. And there are blessed moments when God's truth comes to bear and you see grace in action. Don't pay undue attention to zigzag. Look at the overall direction. If the direction is Godward, you are serving and leading in a way that honors Him.

ENDNOTES

[1] See chapter 21, "Taking Sufficient Care of Ourselves."
[2] See the case made in this book's introduction.
[3] See chapter 4, "Why Do People Seek Counseling?"

CHAPTER 9

RECOGNIZING MENTAL
ILLNESS AND MAKING
EFFECTIVE REFERRALS

The Bible includes little direct comment on—or description of—mental illness. 1 Samuel 21:10–15 reports that David "changed his behavior before them and pretended to be insane" so that the men of Gath wouldn't kill him. King Achish described him as "mad" after David "made marks on the doors of the gate and let his spittle run down his beard." Distressingly, Jesus's family thought Him to be "out of his mind" as He was thronged with followers (Mark 3:20–21). In John 10:20, Jesus's critics said of Him, "He has a demon and is insane"

In 2 Corinthians 5:13, Paul uses a common metaphor to assert his rationality as he describes himself as a minister of reconciliation: "For if we are beside ourselves, it is for God; if we are not in our right mind, it is for you." Festus infamously said to Paul, "Paul, you are out of your mind; your great learning is driving you out of your mind" (Acts 26:24–29). We love Paul's calm and measured response: "I am not out of my mind, most excellent Festus, but I am speaking true and rational words."

While the Bible offers no definition of mental illness, it offers some clues. Mental illness can include behavior deemed abnormal within a given social context. It can include actions that are considered extreme. It sometimes includes words or actions deemed irrational.[1]

A practical modern definition states, "Mental illness is a disease that causes disturbances in thinking, perception, or behavior which significantly impair a person's ability to cope with life."[2] To a major degree, recognition of mental illness depends on our worldview, our understanding of societal norms, and our knowledge of an individual's usual range of function. With apologies for the use of the word "crazy" (it remains rude and insensitive to speak of the mentally ill as crazy), the following Matchbox 20 lyrics are brilliant.

> I'm not crazy, I'm just a little unwell. I know right now you can't tell; but stay a while and maybe then you'll see a different side of me. I'm not crazy, I'm just a little impaired. I know right now you don't care, but soon enough you're gonna think of me and how I used to be ... me.

The lyrics are an appeal for understanding and contextualization. "Please don't label me. Please take the time to see me as an individual. Please know that my current struggle may not be permanent. I'm aware that something is different, and I'm looking for better." Though written from a non-religious perspective, they even wisely imply that each of us can and should choose to care about others. We use these lyrics in counseling classes because they offer a kind and caring perspective from which to broach the subject of mental illness.

The intersection of Christianity and mental illness remains challenging and complicated. Some Christians find that statement offensively false. In their judgment, mental illness does not exist. They believe secular "experts" invented the concept in an attempt to abolish moral standards and personal responsibility as part of a campaign to undermine the need for all things religious. To this group, the concept of a "mental disease" is viewed as nonsensical; a person might have a disease of the brain—the physical organ, but it is impossible to have a disease of the mind.

Other Christians acknowledge the reality of mental illness but attribute it directly to Satan or sin. We say "directly" in acknowledgment that the world was created flawless. In a forensic sense, there was no disease or flaw until sin occurred and virtually everything changed. Though seldom expressed this bluntly, the concept is, "Mental illness afflicts only those weak in faith and character. You can't be afflicted unless you 'give in to it.'" Some link certain metal illnesses to demon possession as described in the New Testament (Matt 8:28–34, Mark 9:14–29). Some may even link mental health challenges with punishment for sin. We do not.

Some Christians acknowledge the reality of mental illness but never discuss the subject due to stigma and awkwardness. Perhaps you have seen public service statements that seek to destigmatize mental illness. Both silence and ignorance seem poor options in cultures that are medically and psychologically aware.

Historically, Christians have been known for loving efforts to care for the mentally ill and their families. Many such efforts have been institutional in nature and have focused on care for the severely ill. From a modern context, institutional care is seen as a regrettable option of last resort. More recently, strong emphasis has been given to churches meeting the needs of the mentally ill and their families in the local context.[3]

In our judgment, most Christians acknowledge the reality of mental illness even as we lament the politicization of what some have called the psychopharmaceutical mental health industry. Ministerial education routinely includes courses in pastoral counseling. Pastoral counseling courses routinely include instructional units covering the basics of mental illness. In more educated cultures, church members expect a degree of knowledge and understanding of mental illness from their leaders. They expect a degree of recognition when they say, "My mom is battling OCD," or "I need you to know that Dad started taking Zoloft last week."

The expectations of members regarding mental illness awareness can be challenging. They may mention "OCD" and then wait to see if you seem aware of the acronym. If you know they're speaking of obsessive-compulsive disorder, it seems wise to use the full phrase in your reply. If you don't know the acronym or it "hides" from you in the moment, our recommendation is to ask them what they mean. The bigger recommendation is "never fake it." If you don't know, ask them to educate you.

You may know from TV commercials or general experience that Zoloft is the name brand of a common antidepressant. When they say, "Dad started taking Zoloft last week," they have told you several things. "We recognize that Dad needs help with his depression. We are willing to accept medical as well as spiritual help. It's important to us for you to know these things." And the next question we hope you ask yourself is, "Why is it important to them for me to know this? How am I going to be part of their helping team?"

Perhaps you have read some version of the following in popular media: "Over their lifespan, 70% of US citizens will face a mental illness," and "One in five US adults will face a mental illness during any given year." Regrettably, such statements are often non-nuanced. They do not explain that "mental illness" covers huge and diverse territory from relatively mild depression and anxiety to major psychotic disorders. Thankfully, the vast majority of mental illnesses fall on the lower end of that continuum. Why do we cite these potentially alarming statistics? As church leaders, we will deal with the mentally ill and their families. It's not a matter of if, but of when. Our goal is to be prepared to help to the degree that we are able—and to protect ourselves from both unrealistic expectations and harmful actions.

A MAJOR CAVEAT

We would be stunningly unfair to imply that church leaders must be experts in the recognition and treatment of mental illness. We would never suggest that church leaders try to master the *Diagnostic and Statistical Manual of Mental Disorders*, i.e. DSM-5.[4] The book is quite technical, and the terminology is ever-changing.

We do, however, recommend basic awareness of the major categories of disorders: schizophrenia spectrum, bipolar, depressive, anxiety, obsessive-compulsive, trauma and stressor-related, feeding and eating, substance-related and addictive, and personality. Our listing is somewhat arbitrary, including approximately half the disorders listed in DSM-5.

It would be helpful to know that people diagnosed within the schizophrenia spectrum and other psychotic disorders as well as bipolar disorder will be prescribed appropriate medication. One of the best services we can offer those individuals and their families is to remind them, "Please stay medically compliant. Take your medications as prescribed, don't stop taking them, and don't mix them with alcohol or other drugs." When people have concerns about the medications, advise them to discuss those concerns with their doctors. A key rule for those of us who are not doctors: Never give medical advice.

Those with psychotic disorders often function well when they are medically compliant. If they stop the medication, their behavior often changes dramatically. They may hear voices, see things that don't exist, forego personal hygiene practices, or become highly dysfunctional. Our recommendation is to work with their family to get them back on track with their medical team.

Often as church leaders, we don't interact directly with the severely ill; our work is with their families. Our key roles are love, support, and reassurance. "Yes, we are aware that your family member is ill. We still love her, and we will always love you. As Christians, we are family.

We are blessed that you work and worship with us. We are here for you."

Those diagnosed with less severe disorders may be prescribed medication as well. Some disorders are most effectively addressed through behavioral therapy—phobias for example. For depressive disorders, the data overwhelmingly indicate that the most effective treatment is a combination of medication and counseling. A general knowledge of standard treatment protocols is not essential but can be helpful. At our level of helping, the following information may be of more immediate and practical value.

When working with families who are less medically/psychologically aware, church leaders are often asked, "Is this illness genetic? Will it happen to me?" We dare not say more than is proper, but we recommend the following responses:

- "Many mental illnesses have a genetic component. Please know that genetic linkage is never lock-step. Having a statistically stronger likelihood to develop a disorder does not guarantee that the disorder will develop."
- "Talk with your doctors. Often there is strong interaction between environmental factors and genetic predisposition. Ask your doctor, 'Are there lifestyle choices I can make (diet, exercise, stress management, etc.) that can lower the likelihood of this illness?'"
- "Live in awareness, but not in dread. Self-monitor, but don't let what may never happen take control of your life."

When working with family members of the mentally ill, you may be asked, "Why do people treat our whole family differently? Why do they treat us like we have some contagion?" Certainly, mental illnesses are not contagious, but they are scary. Again, we recommend expressions of love and appreciation. Express your respect for their courage and compassion. As appropriate, express that respect to others. Look for ways to connect and encourage. Be sure to include these families in your personal hospitality and fellowship.

As leaders, you may encounter a different level of questions about severe mental illness. Under-informed church members may ask, "I hear Bill has a major mental illness. Is he dangerous? Is it wise for you to let him keep worshiping with us? Who knows what he might do?" From our counseling perspective, it's a challenge not to bristle at such questions, but education is the need in such moments. Scary movies aside, statistics indicate that members of the general population are more likely to harm others than are mentally ill individuals. Those battling mental disorders are more likely to harm themselves than others, and even this occurs infrequently, statistically speaking. Fear of the mentally ill is largely fear born of ignorance.

Numerous categories of mental illness categorized within DSM-5 lie beyond our ability to offer targeted, direct help. While love, listening, prayer, friendship, kindness, gentleness, and respect are always virtuous, God does not give us curative power. Several warnings are needed.

As powerful as prayer is, we would be most unwise to declare a person "sufficiently helped" just because we have prayed. If a person came in with a serious bleeding wound, we'd pray as we called 911. If a person described an alarming lump that might be a tumor, we'd pray as we encouraged seeing the best available doctor. The same common-sense principles apply to mental illness.

As powerful as truth is, we would be most unwise to tell a person battling bulimia, "Just stop the binge-and-purge cycle. Give me your word that you won't do that anymore." We'd be just as naive to tell a person battling anorexia nervosa, "You have to promise me that you'll eat three meals every day from now on." These powerful disorders cannot be overcome by willpower. The dynamics in play are too strong and too complex. Referral to a professional is essential.

As powerful as the Bible is, we would be most unwise to tell a person battling anxiety, "I want you to read Matthew 6:25–34 twice a day every day. If you'll do that and obey Jesus's command not to worry, you'll be fine from now on." Oh, that it was so simple! Reading the good book and striving to obey is blessed and will bless. Do not downplay or fail to employ Scripture, but give the person you are helping multiple options for improvement and multiple opportunities for success.

Ask the anxious person, "Have you always felt this anxious? Were there times in your life when anxiety did not plague you? Has something happened to trigger your anxiety? If so, have you seen this trigger before?"

Ask, "What behaviors accompany your anxiety? Are they helping you cope, or are they making things worse? What options are available? What might you do differently? Are you ever able to battle the anxiety through distraction and refocusing? Have you been able to break an anxious episode by changing your location (going outside), by changing your environment (happy music, playing with your dog), or by changing your focus (I'm taking ten minutes to pray right now)?"

Ask, "When you feel anxious, what do you tell yourself? What messages play in your head? Are these messages true or false? Helpful or unhelpful? Do you know that you can choose the messages that you believe?"

EFFECTIVE REFERRAL

When we recognize that a person needs help at a level we can't provide, how do we help? First, we tell the truth. We remind ourselves and the person in need, "I love you. I want to help you any way that I can, but your need is greater than my knowledge and skills. We're going to need a team." Please notice the affirmation and reassurance. "I'm not dismissing you. I'm not refusing to help. I'm going to be part of your ongoing team if you want me to be." Please notice the positivity, the hope. "Your need is greater than my knowledge and skills, but we have options. We're not giving up."

To whom do you refer? We recommend that our ministry students make a list of mental health options within their respective locations. Is there a Christian psychiatrist—a medical doctor who specializes in mental health? If not, is there a psychiatrist or psychologist who is spiritually safe—one who is not hostile toward faith? Sometimes identifying a neutral partner is as good as it gets.

If the need is lesser, are there Christian counselors in

the area? Do they have specializations? Do they have room for additional clients? Do they accept insurance? If not, are they affordable? Any team-building options that we offer need to be realistic, and that includes financial affordability. Thus, we suggest two caveats for consideration.

First, might the church be willing to assist financially? Our recommendation is to discuss this before an emergency need arises. Treatment for mental illness can be stunningly expensive. Create a flexible and realistic policy. Decide in advance what you can and cannot promise. Do not over-promise. If you can help, be clear about the terms and conditions of your help.

Second, some people who have insurance that would cover mental health needs do not want to use that insurance. For certain jobs with security clearance, having an official mental health diagnosis could be career ending. Referral gets complicated. The best policy is to provide options and make suggestions without mandating.

MENTAL ILLNESS MYTHS

The most common misconceptions regarding mental illness have no basis in reality, but they are pervasive and stubborn.

Myth 1: Mental disorders strike only weak (ignorant or faithless or lazy) people. In truth, mental disorders know no age, class, ethnic, religious, or educational bounds.

Myth 2: Mental disorders are contagious. Review the discussion above.

Myth 3: People with mental disorders cannot function within society. Millions function quite well with appropriate treatment and support systems.

Myth 4: Once mentally ill, always mentally ill. This myth is patently false. For some people, the stigma of mental illness remains forever. This is a clear violation of Matthew 7:12, John 13:34-35, and Philippians 2:1-4.

Myth 5: Mental illness will go away if we just ignore it. Apply common sense; how often do major life challenges just fix themselves?

Myth 6: Children are immune to mental illness. There is huge debate about over-diagnosis with children, particularly of Attention Deficit Hyper-Activity Disorder, but unqualified immunity does not exist.

Myth 7: A person can have only one mental illness at a given time. In truth, multiple diagnoses are not uncommon.

Myth 8: A non-professional cannot help a person with a mental disorder. Clearly, there are limits to our ability to help. Certain disorders are fiercely resistant to help at even the highest levels of education and competency. However, the vast majority of people value and benefit from a caring heart and a listening ear. Virtually everyone benefits from being engaged, acknowledged, and treated like a person—unique, individual, and made in the image of God. And as Christian leaders, we have the added opportunity to love each person with the love of the Lord.

ENDNOTES

[1.] For a detailed discussion of the Bible and mental

illness, see Christopher C. H. Cook, *The Bible and Mental Health: Towards a Biblical Theology of Mental Health* (Louisville: Westminster John Knox Press, 2020). Also, Matthew S. Stafford. *Grace for the Afflicted: A Clinical and Biblical Perspective on Mental Illness* (Downers Grove: InterVarsity Press, 2017).

2. Source unknown, but not original with these authors.

3. See Jessica Brown, *Making Room at the Well: Mental Health and the Church* (Valley Forge, PA: Judson Press, 2020). Stephen Grcevich, *Mental Health and the Church: A Ministry Handbook for Including Children and Adults with ADHD, Anxiety Mood Disorders, and Other Common Mental Health Conditions* (Grand Rapids: Zondervan, 2017). Tim Clinton, *The Struggle Is Real: How to Care for Mental and Relational Health Issues in the Church* (Bloomington, IN: Author Solutions, 2017).

4. American Psychiatric Association, *Diagnostic and Statistical Manual of Mental Disorders.* 5th ed. (Arlington, VA: American Psychiatric Association: 2013).

CHAPTER 10
HELPING THE ANGRY

From domestic violence to road rage to general incivility, we live in an angry world. As church leaders our approach to helping the angry must flow from Scripture. It seems wise to begin this chapter with a review of biblical teaching on anger. What we don't know can hurt us. What we "know" that isn't really true can do even greater harm. As we work to help others, we're ethically obligated to offer the best and wisest of assistance.

ANGER IS NEITHER INHERENTLY BAD NOR SINFUL

Anger is a broad and flexible emotion, neither good nor bad within itself. The clearest proof that anger can be non-sinful is the biblical revelation that God feels and displays anger (Exod 4:14, 25:3-4, 32:10, 13, 14). Jesus displayed anger on occasion (Mark 3:1-5, John 2:13-17).

Anything that God exhibits cannot be inherently wrong (Jas 1:16, 1 Pet 1:13–16).

Careful reading of Ephesians 4:26–27 also helps us. The passage implicitly teaches that anger can lead to sin, but anger itself is not always sinful. This knowledge has practical value when we attempt to help angry people. Sometimes their need is not help with the anger but with the guilt they feel due to self-condemnation. They have been wrongly taught that it's always sinful to feel anger, so their consciences afflict them when they do. Knowing the truth of God's word can immediately set us free from false guilt. Common sense also helps here. Who wouldn't rightly feel anger when seeing a puppy being kicked, a child being verbally abused, or a friend being harmed by a lie?

ANGER IS OFTEN ASSOCIATED WITH BOTH DANGER AND SIN

While Ephesians 4 differentiates sin and anger, it also hints at their frequent, strong connection. Ephesians 4:31 urges that bitterness, wrath, and anger "be put away." Clearly, there are sinful categories of anger (Gal 5:19–21). Scripture associates extreme anger with Cain's murder of Abel (Gen 4:5). In anger, King Saul launched a spear in an attempt to kill his own righteous son (1 Sam 20:24–34). In anger, the mob "ground their teeth" at Stephen before stoning him (Acts 7:54–60). Proverbs 14:29 links anger and folly. Proverbs 15:18 links anger and contention. Proverbs 19:19 links anger and punishment. Proverbs 29:22 links anger with strife and transgression. "Anger lodges in the bosom of fools" (Eccl 7:9). Anger puts us in danger of judgment (Matt 5:22). Anger often shuts down thinking and brings out the worst in us.

Thus, the Bible strongly recommends being slow to anger (Jas 1:19–20; Prov 14:29). Being slow to anger is linked to "great understanding" and good sense (Prov 19:11). "Whoever is slow to anger is better than the mighty, and he who rules his spirit than he who takes a city" (Prov 16:32). Being slow to anger is an attribute of God (Nah 1:3). Who doesn't have a story of quick anger that led to embarrassment or harm? We think of broken windows, broken hands, and broken relationships.

ANGER CAN BE LEARNED

"Make no friendship with a man given to anger, nor go with a wrathful man, lest you learn his ways and entangle yourself in a snare" (Prov 22:24–25). What insightful teaching! On one level, it's 1 Corinthians 15:33 on steroids. We tend to become like those with whom we associate. On another level, it's a reminder that anger can be learned.

A word of caution is in order. Anger as an emotion is what it is—a feeling that can comes in a millisecond. It comes without warning. Anger as a set of behavioral choices is notably different. Many people don't differentiate the two. They unwisely view an angry feeling and their behavioral response as lockstep or innate. They become the Hulk, and they believe they can't help it. Both Proverbs 22:24–25 and common sense beg to differ. One person feels great anger and is moved to prayer while another is moved to profanity. One is moved to rescue, but another is moved to retaliation. One is moved to tears while another is moved to "tear up the world." When we work to help the angry, it's powerful to know that person has a habitual or preferred set of anger responses. Many don't realize that they've learned this response set, and they don't know that they have the option of learning a better one. Even if they have learned the ways of "a man given to anger," they can upgrade. They can choose to learn the ways of a Man given to peace (Isa 9:6). One clear implication for helping an angry person is that helping is likely to involve major teaching.

Proverbs 22:24–25 offers an additional insight regarding those who are "given to anger." Such people are a danger to themselves and to others. While not beyond help, such people are difficult to help. Perpetual anger is woven into the fabric of their being. For many, that happened because they have endured harm and anger since birth. For others, anger is their key means of self-preservation. Others have seen anger effectively used both in self-defense and selfishness. They use anger because it works. Fair warning—helping such people will be slow and labor intensive. On the positive side, there's no heart that God can't change provided the heart is willing.

An additional note: It is not always important to know why a person is "given to anger." Some can recognize that fact and choose to change without the need to examine causation. Others can't. For some, exploring causation—"Why am I like this?"—is crucial. There can be no peace without an answer. We recommend following the lead of the person being helped. If no exploration is needed, don't explore. If exploration is needed, invest the time and energy. When helping people, it's never "one size fits all."

BENEFITS OF ANGER

Righteous anger shows that our beliefs are biblical and our moral compass is intact (John 2:13-17, Neh 13:23-37). Anger tells us that something needs attention; something needs correction. It's a call to action.

Also, anger is energy—admittedly raw energy in need of processing. One of the biggest questions regarding anger is "What should I do with this energy?" We've all heard it before: "I'm so angry, I don't know what to do. If I don't do something, I'm going to explode!" Not to miss the hyperbole, exploding makes a terrible mess. Is there a way to channel the anger? Is there a way to use the energy for good? Is there a way to use this anger to grow personally, to serve others, and to honor God?

I remember as a child on the farm, my dad told us that he was going to use dynamite to uproot stumps along a tree line between two fields. We'd seen movies. This was going to be great with thundering noise, billowing smoke, and huge oak stumps tumbling through the air. He let us go watch from a safe distance. He used an iron rod—I think the axle from a ancient car—to poke a hole under the biggest stump. The dynamite was placed and the fuse lit. We covered our ears, so ready for the BOOM! But the boom was a dull thud, there was no smoke, and the stump barely shook; but when the tractor came to move it, it rolled away with ease.

That's our goal with the energy of anger—channel it,

harness it, and direct it. Use it purposefully to accomplish a worthy goal.

HOW DO WE HELP PEOPLE DEAL WITH ANGER?

Please review the section "God with Cain" in the chapter 1 "God as Counselor." Genesis 4 reminds us that God intervened when He saw that Cain was in danger. God took the initiative. In doing so, He did not allow the situation to worsen before attempting to help.

God intervened with a series of questions. As we work to help people deal with anger, the following questions, if posed lovingly and with humility, could be of help.

- **Do you know why you're angry?** A caveat: because many Christians believe anger to be a sin, they resist admitting it. They deny or mislabel. We will always remember the angry husband who went rigid, tuned red-faced, and yelled, "WHY DO YOU THINK I'M ANGRY? I'M NOT ANGRY!" Sometimes when facing such denial, it's best not to argue. Let the person being helped label his or her emotions. Give the process time to work. Don't be suckered into an argument over the definition of terms. Not every battle will be won today.
- **At whom are you angry?** There's great danger in assuming. They could be angry at themselves, at God, at another person, at the

situation, or at any combination thereof. They may not know. We don't know until they tell or show us.

- **Are you proportionately angry?** Is the level of your anger proper for the gravity of the situation? Sadly, some people have only two anger settings, angry and not angry. They choose to feel the same level of pain and rage over a broken teacup as over a broken heart. In such cases, we'll be teaching about nuance, fine tuning, moderation, and good judgment.
- **Are you aware of how anger affects you?** Does your volume increase? Does your heartrate climb? Do you move toward fight or flight?
- **Do you realize that, angry or not, you're still in control of and responsible for your words and actions?** No, we won't ask this question in just this way. It may be that we don't ask it at all, except in our own minds. But the answer matters. The classic form of the destructive denial of responsibility goes like this: "I'm a calm person. I'm easy going. It takes a lot to rile me. But don't rile me. I'm not responsible for what happens once you push me too far." We must challenge such errant self-talk. It never leads to grace and peace.
- **What is your normal (usual, habitual, preferred) response to anger?** When you become angry, what do you do? The follow-up question is "And how has that worked for

you?" An even better question is "Is your usual response in keeping with your love for Christ?" We know of only four categories of anger response:

1. Anger can be stuffed, internalized, stored inside. If stored at sufficient pressure and/or toxicity for sufficient time, it either escapes by explosion, or it eats out and destroys the person who is storing it.
2. As discussed above, anger can be denied, hidden, or otherwise mislabeled. Denial of reality is denial of truth. It doesn't work well for anyone, especially for Christians.
3. Anger can be released explosively. From verbal to physical violence, its destructive power is legendary.
4. Anger can be processed and directed toward God's service and personal growth.

What are the purposes of such questions? We ask in order to gain enough understanding to offer competent help. We ask to create a climate of inquiry, of guided discovery, so the person battling anger can gain awareness and understanding. We want our angry friend to discover personal strengths that can be used to moderate excessive anger, paving the path for godly choices. Discovering strengths has the added benefit of helping the person feel rewarded for doing the difficult work of anger management. We ask to offer the angry person an opportunity to slow down, to avoid catastrophizing, and to consider more godly options. We ask to show that we care.

We offer help through asking appropriate questions, and we offer help by modeling calmness. Our rule of thumb: The angrier the person we're helping, the calmer we remain. The louder the person we're helping, the more softly we speak. The more animated the angry person, the more gentle we become. This "rule" flows from Proverbs 15:1: "A soft answer turns away wrath, but a harsh word stirs up anger." When dealing with anger, if we fight fire with fire, everyone gets burned. Anger cannot be defeated at its own level. If we can limit the situation to just one angry person at a time, that, in itself, is a partial victory.

Again, a caveat is in order. It is difficult to remain calm in the face of fierce anger. At times, when we're trying to help, we will feel anything but calm. That's part of being human. In such situations, it's imperative that we act better than we feel. Some will label that hypocrisy. It isn't. This isn't about bad motives, manipulation, or intent to deceive. Acting better than we feel flows from love, maturity, and good judgment. It's modeling the very self-control that we're trying to teach and recommend.

WHAT ABOUT VENTING?

Venting is at least a two-edged sword. On the positive side, venting can be cathartic. It can let angry people "get it off their chest" and feel less pressured. With no desire to excuse evil speaking, angry words spoken to a safe person are far less harmful than angry attacks on unsafe people.

On the other hand, venting has the opposite effect for some. The more they talk the angrier they get. The more they talk the more the offense grows and the more justified they feel in retaliation. Even when expressing pain for the sake of healing, Ephesians 4:29–33 offers powerful guidance. Expressing pain for the sake of justifying ungodly actions is a lose-lose proposition.

It's legitimate to ask: "When I'm helping angry people, how will I know whether their venting is helpful or harmful, godly or ungodly?" Sorry, but we won't always know. On the blessed side, most of us gain a degree of skill through experience.

We can offer three recommendations. Does the venting border on raving? If it does, it is unlikely to help. Attempt to redirect the individual to a wiser form of expression.

It's equally legitimate to ask, "Does the venting involve catastrophizing?" For example, "This is the worst thing ever. I can't believe they did this. Not even Job suffered like I'm suffering." There's no blessing in catastrophizing.

Third, is the venting nuanced? Does it include a degree of balance? Signs of balance include statements like: "I know the people who hurt me aren't all bad; I know they have their good qualities. I know I may have contributed to this situation. I could have handled things better." Nuanced venting exhibits grace and fairness. It tends toward health and healing.

TECHNIQUES THAT CAN HELP WITH ANGER

We would never diminish or circumvent Matthew 18:15–20. Clear, honest, loving, face to face conflict resolution is the Lord's way. Regrettably, that isn't always possible. For example, anger flows from unresolved conflict with a person who is no longer living. While Matthew 18 cannot be implemented under that circumstance, the spirit of the text can be honored. The principle taught by Jesus can be observed. How? One time-honored technique is to write a letter expressing the anger, documenting the pain, and then offering forgiveness in the spirit of Luke 23:34 and Acts 7:60. Once the letter has been written, cried over, and prayed over, it can be shredded. Better yet, it can be burned in a safe manner so that the release of pain and anger is symbolized by the ascending smoke.

The Empty Chair Technique is also time-honored and safe. When the person who created (or helped originate) the pain and anger cannot be physically present in the room, "put" that person in an empty chair. To be blunt, pretend. Use a bit of imagination. We have seen this work beautifully. The person battling anger chooses to speak to the source of their pain as if that person were present. As with the letter, the anger is stated and the pain is described. Then, there's a willing statement of forgiveness and release.

A reminder is in order. You may be helping a person who was the source of pain and anger. It may be that the person they harmed is now dead or unwilling to allow a face to face meeting. Both the letter or the Empty Chair Technique can still work with great effectiveness. We acknowledge that this sounds a bit weird at first, but we have seen it greatly bless many. In our judgment, both these techniques are low risk with the opportunity for excellent reward.

THE REALITY OF ANGER

Anger is a part of life in this sin-damaged world. A person who asserts, "I never get angry," isn't showing wisdom. It's wise to admit our own anger for many reasons. All humans sin, so all of us are what some have described as wounded healers. That gives us humility and establishes our common humanity.

While we acknowledge that we are all wounded healers, we also recognize the principle that "hurt people hurt people." Often people who have suffered trauma, either intentionally or unintentionally, harm others either by perpetuating the trauma or letting the scars of their pain limit our effectiveness. We don't say this to scare church leaders or to invite them not to help in Jesus's name.

What is the purpose of this acknowledgment? We who have been blessed, forgiven, and healed by Jesus are uniquely equipped to offer help to others. We know where we have been and what we have done. We also know what God has done for us. And we want to be instruments of His grace in helping others. An angry person can't be well-served by another angry person. But a person whom God has blessed can be a major blessing to all who are willing. We don't deny our own struggles or the victories that God has given us. We use both in His service.

CHAPTER 11
HELPING THE DEPRESSED

But he [Elijah] himself went a day's journey into the wilderness and came and sat down under a broom tree. And he asked that he might die, saying, "It is enough, now, O LORD, take away my life, for I am no better than my fathers." And he lay down and slept under a broom tree (1 Kings 19:4–5a).

Elijah had just experienced an amazing victory over the prophets of Baal. God had shown His power and supported Elijah in the showdown with Baal's prophets; so how did Elijah end up sitting alone under a broom tree wanting to die? How could this man of God with such strong faith be so depressed and in despair?

Let's try to understand. Depression is one of the most common mental disorders in the world. Each year about 3 million Americans will be diagnosed with depression. Current research indicates that it is caused by a combination of genetic, biological, environmental, and psychological factors.[1]

Depression is a clinical term that is not used in the Bible. However, a search of scripture indicates that depression, described with other terms, was a common problem dating back to Old Testament times. Many Psalms (including 43, 69, 88, and 102) deal with despair, but also offer hope. In addition to Elijah and David, others' struggles with despair are recounted in scripture. Jeremiah (Jer 20:14, 18) wrote an entire book of lamentations. Job (Job 1:20; 2:9, 13; 3:11, 26; 10:1; 30:15–17), Moses (Exod 32:32), Jonah (Jonah 4:3, 9), and Peter (Luke 22:55–62) all had experience with depression. When facing His eminent death in the garden, Jesus dealt with grief and anxiety (Matt 26:38; Mark 14:34–36; Luke 22:44). All these had hope and experienced positive resolution of the circumstances surrounding their depression. But there is an infamous instance of unresolved sorrow and remorse: Judas (Matt 27:3–5).

Church leaders will have many occasions to help those who are dealing with depression. What do we learn from scripture about how to cope with depression? What can we do to help a depressed person?

First and foremost, PRAY! Elijah, David, Jonah and others talked to God about what they were experiencing as well as their needs and desires. They didn't always have immediate success, but because they sought God, He was with them and helped them learn and grow through the difficult times.

Contrast those characters with Judas. It seems Judas was filled with remorse, but rather than turning to God, Judas went back to his co-conspirators to return the money. Matthew tells us Judas "changed his mind." We've all made decisions or taken actions we regretted.

We start looking for a way to undo what has been done. We want a rewind. Judas regretted his decision and actions, but he went to the priests, not to God, with his confession and regret. Judas found no solace from the priests. When he found no successful resolution to his remorse, he turned to suicide. We must remember what Judas forgot: seeking God's will and His guidance is always the most important step.

The second way to help is to encourage the depressed person to take care of his/her physiological health. In the story of Elijah's depression, we see the attention given to care for Elijah's physiological needs. God provided him with food and water. Elijah ate and slept; then he was rejuvenated.

As non-medical helpers, we cannot alter someone's genetic or biological make up, but there are some things that can be done to improve physiological functioning. Lack of sleep, lack of exercise, physical illness and/or pain, improper diet, vitamin deficiencies, abuse of drugs and alcohol, and side effects of some medications can contribute to depression. Of course we would *never* suggest someone change or discontinue medication. We could suggest a depressed person discuss his/her medications with his/her healthcare provider. There are also psychotropic medications that can improve the functioning of the nervous system, resulting in an improvement in coping and thinking. Those medications must be prescribed by a health care professional.

Within the scope of what we can do is to suggest changes to improve the physiological factors that are within an individual's control. For example, getting sufficient sleep, eating properly, and exercising are all things that can be done by the individual. Discuss the importance of avoiding alcohol and drugs, which may exacerbate their depression. It is a good idea to encourage the depressed person to get a thorough physical exam. Many physical disorders and conditions can contribute to depression. For example, if someone's thyroid is malfunctioning, no amount of counseling or concern can alter the impact of hyperthyroidism or hypothyroidism. A physical exam and proper medications or other medical interventions can be the solution. Encourage depressed persons to get a physical exam and blood work.

The third area in which church leaders could offer help or influence is in the cognitive (or thinking) causes of depression. It is rare that a person makes an immediate turnaround from depression. Most often, recovery from depression is a long difficult journey with many ups and downs. Telling someone, "Just don't feel that way," or "Stop thinking like that," does nothing to help the depressed person. Such statements will probably add feelings of guilt and self-blame since most people cannot change how they feel just by desiring to change. Some Christians believe they should always be joyful and enthusiastic, so when discouragement and anger occur, they feel like failures who have displeased God, and that feeling contributes to their depression. What can church leaders do or say to help and not add to someone's despair?

(1) Help them learn to trust God. Through many difficult circumstances, Paul learned to be content (Phil 4:11). Trusting God allows us to be content when things are difficult. If as church leaders we can guide others to

learn this, their ability to cope when difficulty comes will be enhanced.

(2) Understand that situations will arise in the lives of members of our congregations when feelings of sadness are an appropriate response. As helpers we want to offer support to prevent these times from spiraling down to depression. The death of a loved one or the anniversary of that loss, holidays, and other occasions can trigger bouts of depression. During those times people may need extra encouragement and understanding if they are to avoid slipping into depression (Heb 10:24–25, 1 Pet 4:10, Gal 6:9–10),

(3) Gaining control over thinking is an important part of avoiding or recovering from depression. Psychiatrist Aaron Beck writes that depressed people have a negative view of life, a negative view of themselves, and a negative view of the future.[2] Negative thinking causes depression, and depression causes negative thinking. To help someone overcome depression, helpers can stimulate more positive thoughts and develop hope for a better future. Scripture abounds with hope for a better future and with encouragement to control thoughts and meditation. "Rejoice in the lord always; again I will say rejoice" (Phil 4:4).

> Finally, brothers, whatever is true, whatever is honorable, whatever is just, whatever is pure, whatever is lovely, whatever is commendable, if there is any excellence, if there is anything worthy of praise, think about these things (Phil 4:8–9).

> "Peace I leave with you; my peace I give to you. Not

as the world gives do I give to you. Let not your hearts be troubled, neither let them be afraid" (John 14:27).

The *Diagnostic and Statistical Manual of Mental Disorders-5* lists the following criteria for the diagnosis of depression. The individual must have experienced at least 5 of the symptoms for at least two weeks. At least one of the symptoms must be (1) depressed mood or (2) loss of interest or pleasure.

1. Depressed mood most of the day, nearly every day.
2. Diminished interest or pleasure in all, or almost all activities most of the day, nearly every day.
3. Weight loss when not dieting or weight gain, or decrease or increase in appetite nearly every day.
4. A slowing down of thought and a reduction of physical movement (observable by others).
5. Fatigue or loss of energy nearly every day.
6. Feelings of worthlessness or excessive or inappropriate guilt nearly every day.
7. Diminished ability to think or concentrate, or indecisiveness, nearly every day.
8. Recurrent thoughts of death, recurrent suicidal ideation without a specific plan, or a suicide attempt or specific plan for committing suicide.[3]

For many helpers, the danger of suicide elicits a tremendous amount of stress and anxiety. The threat of suicide is greatest among those suffering from depression. Depression distorts thinking, causing someone to do things they would never consider when they are thinking clearly. As we discuss the potential for suicide, let's use the definitions of terms used by the National Institute of Mental Health.

- **Suicide** is defined as death caused by self-directed injurious behavior with intent to die as a result of the behavior.
- **Suicide attempt** is a non-fatal, self-directed injurious behavior with intent to die as a result of the behavior. A suicide attempt might not result in injury.
- **Suicidal ideation** refers to thinking about, considering or planning suicide.[4]

Substance Abuse and Mental Health Services Administration (SAMHSA), a division of the U.S. Department of Health and Human Services, reports that in the United States in 2019:

- 12.0 million adults had serious thoughts of suicide
- 3.5 million adults made suicide plans
- 1.4 million adults attempted suicide[5]

It is likely leaders will be called on to help someone having suicidal ideation or someone concerned for a family member who is considering suicide, has attempted suicide, or has committed suicide. So, what should we say or not say?

First of all, know possible warning signs of suicide:

- talk of suicide (Most people give direct or indirect statements prior to an attempted suicide.)
- preoccupation with death

- giving away valuable items or prized possessions
- recent neglect of appearance
- cleaning or tidying a room more than usual
- sadness, depression, hopelessness, or lack of energy
- uncontrolled anger
- too much or too little sleep
- a sudden lift in spirits or happiness after a long period of sadness
- withdrawing from friends and family
- apologizing to others for past actions
- taking deadly risks
- actions or words of hopelessness, intense anger, or unexplained happiness[6, 7]

Prior to a suicide attempt, an individual may show some of these signs or he/she may show none of them at all. If we have concerns someone is contemplating suicide, we should ask him/her if self-harm is being considered. If the answer is yes, then take action to make sure the individual is in a safe environment. This may mean at home under supervision or the home of a family member, but it may more likely mean getting the individual to the hospital. We should never let a suicidal person leave our presence. We should drive him to the hospital or other secure, supervised environment. A suicidal person is a danger to himself, but he also can be a danger to others. Emotions have taken control of her decision-making ability. Help him or her to think in concrete, fact-based terms by asking questions that are factual. We may already know the answers, but we are trying to change his/her thinking away from emotions. For example: "What time do you have to be at work in the morning? How long have you worked there? What exactly do you do at work?" These questions can be asked as we drive him/her to safety or wait for a family member, ambulance, or law enforcement to come to transport him/her to a safe environment. Keep him/her involved in calm conversation. Work on the underlying causes comes later when he/she are not in a suicidal crisis and thinking is clearer.

In conclusion, sadness, grief, sorrow, depression are all forms of emotional or mental pain. In *The Problem of Pain*, C.S. Lewis wrote,

> Mental pain is less dramatic than physical pain, but it is more common and also more hard to bear. The frequent attempt to conceal mental pain increases the burden: it is easier to say 'My tooth is aching' than to say 'My heart is broken.'[8]

Church leaders can be of great service to the broken hearted. When we listen and help, we are showing Christ's love—not only to the individual but to the world around him or her.

> And when did we see you sick or in prison and visit you? And the King will answer them, "Truly, I say to you, as you did it to one of the least of these, you did it to me" (Matt 25:39-40).

Endnotes

1. National Institute of Mental Health. *Depression: Risk Factors.* http://www.nimh.nih.gov.
2. A.T. Beck, et al., *Cognitive Therapy of Depression* (New York: Guilford, 1979).
3. American Psychiatric Association, *Diagnostic and Statistical Manual of Mental Disorders* 5th *ed.: DSM-5.* (Washington, D.C.: American Psychiatric Association, 2013).
4. National Institute of Mental Health. *Mental Health Information: Statistics.* http://www.nimh.nih.gov
5. Substance Abuse and Mental Health Services Association. *Help Prevent Suicide.* 10/7/2020. http://www.SAMHSA. gov.
6. N.L. Farberow and E.S. Shneidman, eds., *The Cry for Help* (New York: McGraw-Hill, 1965).
7. Suicide and Crisis Center of North Texas, "Warning signs of suicide," https://www.sccenter.org/facts-and-resources/warning-signs/
8. C.S. Lewis, *The Problem of Pain* (United Kingdom, The Centenary Press, 1940, Current edition published by HarperCollins).

CHAPTER 12
HELPING THE FEARFUL

How do we deal with fear? Some Christians know **the biblical answer**, and it's simple. They cite book, chapter, and verse.

- "Though an army encamp against me, my heart shall not fear" (Ps 27:3).
- "Do not fear, only believe" (Mark 9:36).
- "For God gave us a spirit not of fear, but of power and love and self-control" (2 Tim 1:7).
- "The Lord is my helper. I will not fear. What can man do to me?" (Heb 13:7, Ps 118:6)
- "There is no fear in love, but perfect love casts out fear" (1 John 4:18).

They add Revelation 1:17 and 21:8 for good measure. For these bold and confident Christians, fear is failure to take God at His word. Fear is sin, weakness, and lack of faith. Fear is always an unwise, unworthy, and unbiblical choice.

THINKING MORE BROADLY

We're reminded of the famous adage: "For every complex problem [question or issue], there's a solution that is simple, easy, and wrong." The assertions above may be true in some cases; we're blessed to know that facing fear isn't that simple. Fear as an emotion is not sinful. To use an extreme example, there's no sin in fearing snakes or in being startled or distressed when we see one. There would, however, be sin in letting our fear of snakes keep us from rescuing a child who was about to be struck by one.

The idea that only the weak struggle with fear contradicts scripture. There is benefit in remembering that even major biblical characters known for their faith battled fear, and they did not always win the battle. Abraham's fear led to two embarrassing lies (Gen 12:10–20, 20:1–18). Isaac's fear led to a stunningly similar sin (Gen 26:6–11). In fear, David pretended to be mentally ill (1 Sam 21:10–15, Ps 55:1–8). Fear led Peter to deny the Lord, even after being stoutly warned (Matt 26:33–35 & 69–75). Might fear have played a role in the sin of Peter and Barnabas in Galatia (Gal 2:11–18)?

On the other hand, we see good judgment in Israel's fear before the Lord at Sinai (Exod 19:16). Esther's slight delay and prayer request reflected her understanding of the life-and-death situation she was about to face before the king (Esth 4:13–17). While we're amazed at the courage of Shadrach, Meshach, and Abednego, we would never claim that they experienced no fear in the face of the fiery furnace (Dan 3:16–18). Scripture does not describe their emotions, only their faith and commitment to God. How much more courageous their choice if they felt great fear and acted faithfully rather than choosing to preserve their lives!

We do not think poorly of the Philippian jailer who, after earthquake and rescue, "trembling with fear ... fell down before Paul and Silas" (Acts 16:29). In twin acts of healthy transparency, Paul shared his fears with the Corinthian Christians in both 1 Corinthians 2:3 and 2 Corinthians 7:5.

While fear is sometimes warranted, we dare not let it move us to cowardice. John 12:42–43, read with John 7:13 and 9:22, lead many to believe "because of the Pharisees they did not confess Him" must have included an element of fear. If so, this fear certainly set the stage for sin. By not confessing Jesus, they denied Him. Failing to confess Jesus, regardless of the reason, can't be right. Fear—even great fear—offers no excuse for sin (Matt 25:14–30).

HOW DO WE HELP PEOPLE STRUGGLING WITH FEAR?

"Fear" covers extremely broad territory. With this chapter, we do not address fear, particularly fear of God, as a synonym for solemn respect. Classically, a phobia is an extreme or irrational fear. That definition, however, mixes two categories. Extreme rational fears exist— consider a victim of violence whose nemesis remains free, armed, and impenitent. We offer the following as a simple, non-clinical continuum of fear from its mildest form to the highest level:

├─terror extreme aversion
│
│
├─strong sense of danger/threat with major negative life effects
│
│
├─significant sense of danger/threat affecting mood and/or behavior
│
│
├─awareness of concern
│
│
├─light apprehension

In the broadest of terms, it helps to sort fears by category. Some fears are merely inconvenient while others are debilitating. Fear of frogs, clowns, or spiders, for example, may be emotionally troubling, but present no moral danger. Extreme fear of germs or crowds will be life-limiting. Assisting in overcoming phobias may lie outside our skill set, but there are three needed reminders.

Please don't dismiss or make light of phobias. To do so sends a terrible and discouraging message to the victim. Even when we can't offer specific help, we can offer powerful assistance by being caring and respectful.

Secondly, the irrational fear may create an opportunity to teach critical thinking skills. Better thinking leads the individual to better decision-making and to better living.

Finally, we may discover what counselors call "the presenting problem." It may be that the hurting person sought your help and began with mentioning a phobia as a test. The phobia was a safe place to start. There was a need to gauge your level of compassion and wisdom before sharing a deeper and more troubling issue. If it proves to be a test of wisdom and compassion, we're blessed to pass it.

Some fears are rational and others irrational. For irrational fears, those flowing from extremely unlikely events—being struck by a meteor or eaten by piranha, our role may be to listen without laughing or labeling. The need of the moment may be confirmation that we won't judge unbiblically and that God doesn't condemn people just because they struggle.

For rational fears, one of the biggest needs is maintaining truthfulness. Many church leaders feel a strong pull to reassure: "Now, now, everything's going to be okay. God wouldn't let this happen to you or yours." We must avoid offering false reassurance. We dare not make promises that we could not possibly fulfill. Terrible things happened to Abel, Job, Joseph, Jeremiah, Daniel, Naboth, John the Baptizer, and Jesus. When we speak where God has not, we err grievously.

If the fear being addressed is rational, part of our role may lie in risk reduction. Faith does not preclude common sense and good judgment. Can we offer suggestions that minimize the danger? Ideas to explore could include buying a home security system, getting a dog, moving to a safer neighborhood, walking home from work with a friend, or changing shifts at work. We can rightly suggest and offer prayers for protection.

We can recommend comforting biblical passages, including those that document the ability of personal courage to help others overcome fear (Ps 23, John 14, 2 Cor 4–5, Judg 4:4–9, 1 Sam 14:1–14, Phil 1:12–14). And we can share the great biblical truth that the person who fears God ultimately has nothing else to fear (Matt 10:25–33, especially v. 28). We're wise to offer this truth with foundation and compassion rather than as a dismissive platitude. All truth is God's, but some hurting people don't yet have the reservoir of faith and knowledge to hear and grasp His more challenging teachings.

Always, we're wise to listen and learn before forming opinions or offering suggestions. It's possible that a fearful sister has already faced her fear, and like Esther has made a godly choice. It's possible the devil is attacking her through false guilt. "Yes, you did right—eventually. But, you felt fear first. You failed to trust God. You're just as guilty as if you'd never done right." We know this is a lie, but we also know how tenderhearted some people are. A person in this situation needs clarity of thought, compassion, and commendation. A suggested reply: "Bless your tender heart. Being human, you felt fear. Being Christian, you trusted God more than you trusted even your own heart. You chose to honor God by doing what you knew to be right. Your example is so encouraging to me!"

Other scenarios are possible. It could be that our sister has not yet decided to face her fear and do right. She may need help in recognizing that she is not destined to be controlled by her fear. She can act better than she feels. She can do right no matter how she feels. Or she may already know this, but need help in choosing to do what she knows to be best. As counselors, we often lend moral, biblical, and intellectual support to good people. We encourage them to step up to God's will.

Of course, it's possible that our sister has given in to fear and wants help to feel less bad because of her bad decision. "If I can get a church leader to tell me that this is okay, then I won't have to hurt over it anymore." This is help that we can't offer (2 Tim 4:3–4). Doing bad should feel bad. Godly sorrow over sin needs to hold sway and move us to repentance (2 Cor 7:8–12).

First, we listen and learn. Then, we teach. It's so dangerous to assume that everyone knows that the mere feeling of fear, no matter how intense, is not inherently sinful. The devil won't waste effort. If he can persuade a person to believe, "You've already sinned by feeling fear. Since you're already defeated, what you do next doesn't matter," he will take the victory. We're wise to know that our feelings are not fully and immediately under our control. Our actions are. Feelings often flash; they appear from nowhere. Our actions are different; we can always choose to do right.

Knowing that we can and should control our actions is essential, but incomplete. Some people battling fear will need help in identifying options, choosing the best one, and moving from choice to action. For example, it's good to know when we have offended a brother and need to make apology (Matt 5:23–24). To be right with God, we must actually make the apology. Is it best made face to face? Where should it be made? What's the most loving and intelligent timing? We support prayer and sound thinking—provided we don't stop there. To complete the process, the apology must be made sincerely. While we support prayer and sound thinking, we do not support delay. Fear often grows through delay. Unhealthy delay blesses no one.

As we teach and encourage sound biblical thinking, we also encourage accurate assessment. We suggest the following questions for consideration:

- "Have you felt a similar level of fear before? If so, how did the situation turn out? How did you survive it? What did God do to help you?" The concept is to use guided discovery to help the fearful person realize, "I can get through this. God has helped me before, and He will help me again. This situation is not hopeless."
- "If you have felt a similar level of fear before, were any of your fearful feelings exaggerated or extreme? If so, how did you discover that? What did you do about it? Why?" The concept is to invite healthy reflection: "I sometimes catastrophize. This tendency does not bless me. I need to recognize and reject it." Additionally, "I took steps before that helped me. Maybe I need to take those same good steps again."
- "If you have felt a similar level of fear before, what did you do to help yourself? What resources did you access? What blessed you?" The concept is not only to

remember helpful steps taken in the past, but also to remember "I did not do this alone. Other people helped. Certain biblical texts helped. I read some other good material that helped." There is no need to reinvent the wheel if we already know what rolls.

- "If you have not experienced this level of fear before, what has changed? Are you under some new threat or pressure? Has there been a change in your closeness to God? Has there been a negative change in your support system?" The concept is to invite broader assessment. "Have I lost a person who was a pillar in my life? Have I taken a step away from God that diminishes peace and invites fear? Have I started walking by sight and not by faith?"

THREE CAVEATS

Many read Matthew 5:23–24 with Matthew 18:15–17. Because Matthew 18:15 says, "Go and tell him his fault between you and him alone," some conclude that the same applies to Matthew 5:23–24. As church leaders, we will sometimes be asked to accompany a person who wants to right the offense he has committed against a brother. Can we do so biblically?

Our answer: "It depends." We will not be doing God's work if we hinder peace making and reconciliation by becoming the spokesman. "I have sinned" needs to be spoken by the repentant sinner. "Please forgive me" needs to be spoken by the person in need of forgiveness. That dynamic is too powerful to be circumvented.

On the other hand, we can accompany our brother in support of peace, truth, and love (Matt 5:9, Rom 12:18, Phil 4:1–3). There is no biblical mandate to face our fears and challenges alone (Eccl 4:9–12). We love the beautiful balance of Galatians 6:1–5. We help one another stay right and shoulder responsibility. We can't help others by facing their fears or fulfilling their God-given obligations for them.

Secondly, as with most of life, expect progress in overcoming fear to be zigzag. It's far more likely to be a process complete with setbacks rather than a monumental breakthrough when all fear disappears entirely and forever. We don't deny that God is capable of those monumental moments, but we seldom have the capacity to receive that level of blessing.

Finally, "progress" is a very broad word in the context of dealing with fear. In the best of cases, the fear is overcome never to return. Sometimes the fear is largely overcome, but ongoing battles ensue. As the fear tries to return, we battle it with prayer, biblical teaching, sound thinking, and the support of trusted friends.

A REMINDER ABOUT PROGRESS

Sometimes, the fear is not overcome, but it is managed to an effective degree. For Christians this is in no way a denial of Psalm 27:3, Mark 9:36, John 14:27, 2 Timothy 1:7, or Hebrews 13:7. Rather, it's a realistic admission of human frailty in this sin-damaged world. Satan will deny this nuanced view. He will assert that dealing with fear is either/or: "You claim to believe the Bible. Either you trust God by 'casting all your anxieties on Him, because He cares for you' (1 Pet 5:7), or you don't. God doesn't tolerate halfhearted faith." Please note that we present the devil quoting scripture just as he did to Jesus (Matt 4:6). Nothing is sacred to Satan.

Do we see the errors in Satan's statements above? He presents a classic false dichotomy. He presents a situation as either/or when it's far more complex. He omits grace. He subtly denies the great truth taught in Mark 9:14–29. In our better moments, all of us can identify with the desperate father's plea, "I believe, help my unbelief!" (Mark 9:24) We know that we are works in progress. Our faith always needs to grow (2 Cor 10:15, 2 Thess 1:3, 2 Pet 1:5–11). God doesn't bless halfhearted faith, but He has an outstanding history of faith development. He has an outstandingly gracious record of working with those who want His help and blessing (Luke 17:5–6, 22:31–32; John 20:24–31).

TWO RECOMMENDATIONS

When you are blessed to help a fellow Christian overcome any fear, please don't forget commendation and celebration. Tell the overcomer, "I'm so happy for you. I love the victory that God has given you!" And please don't forget to ask, "How do you feel now that God has given you this victory?" We do not imply that our feelings are God's standard, but we love to celebrate with those who open the door of God's deliverance (Rom 12:15, Phil 2:3–4). We want them to use the energy and encouragement of the "win" for even greater spiritual service.

If the victory over fear comes in the form of faithful endurance, please don't forget 2 Corinthians 12:7–10. God didn't remove Paul's thorn, but He changed Paul's perspective. He gave Paul—and us—a lesson in grace, trust, strength, wisdom, power, perspective, and humility. The longer we live, the more we appreciate those deep and quiet souls who face great fear and trust God anyway.

CHAPTER 13
HELPING THE GRIEVING

Grief is universal; it afflicts everyone. Grief is deeply personal; it afflicts each individual uniquely. Most associate grief with the process of coping, surviving, and finding life's "new normal" following a death. Grief is much broader. In some way, on some level, every major loss is grieved. This chapter was written during Covid-19 "stay at home" orders. People were grieving the loss of daily routine, graduation postponement (perhaps cancellation), lost jobs, delayed vacations, and the loss of a sense of safety and control—as well as losses through death. Even in safer times, people grieve divorce, health loss, loss of dreams, and loss of friendships.

As church leaders—even as decent people—we're blessed to know something of the scope of grief. That knowledge can help us keep our feet out of our mouths. A friend loses her auntie, and we find ourselves surprised at the level of her grief. God forbid, but we're tempted to say, "Get a grip. This isn't the end of the world. She was only your aunt." Somehow before those terrible words escape, we're blessed with additional information. The deceased was technically an aunt, but functionally, she was our friend's mother. Without her, our friend doesn't know how she would have survived. With no disrespect to aunts and uncles, this loss isn't "normal." This grief won't be "normal"; it can't be. In many ways, the words "normal" and "grief" never belong in the same sentence.

WHAT PEOPLE DON'T KNOW CAN HURT THEM

Elizabeth Kubler-Ross did pioneering work articulating the stages and describing the nature of grief.[1] Her stages are woven into the fabric of our culture; they're part of conventional wisdom.

Denial. *"This can't be happening. It can't be real. I'll awaken from this nightmare, and it will never have happened."* Some describe it as shock, numbness, entering a fog, or living in extra-slow motion.

Anger. *"This can't happen to me. It can't happen to my family. We've done nothing to deserve this. This isn't fair. This can't be right!"* The anger can be directed toward self, family, first responders, an insurance company, the government, medical professionals, God, or even the person who has died or otherwise been lost.

Bargaining. *"This won't be real if I will only pray enough, believe enough, do enough, suffer enough, promise enough, or ____ enough."* The bargaining is irrational because it's based on erroneous assumptions. Within those assumptions, though, the bargaining feels/seems completely logical.

Depression. See chapter 11 on depression. Depression presents in many conflicting ways, including eating everything/eating nothing, inability to work/inability to stop working, and always sleeping/never being able to sleep.

Acceptance. *"Terrible as it is, it happened. The loss is real and permanent. My work now is to find my new reality and move forward. There may even be ways that I can grow through this."* The victory can't be found in undoing the loss. The victory is surviving it and using what I've learned to help others.

Along with the stages comes the broad assumption that it takes 18 to 24 months to complete the cycle of grief. Talk about urban legends and damaging myths! Grief has neither clock nor calendar. It can't be put on a timetable. The stages of grief may be helpful in the broadest of senses, but they're never helpful if they're viewed as lockstep and linear. People can be in multiple stages at once. Stages can be repeated. Reversion to a previous stage is common. And people battling grief hate to be assigned to what they think of as arbitrary stages. Perhaps we'd be much wiser to discuss the tasks of grieving rather than the stages.

BIBLICAL EXAMPLES OF GRIEF

Jacob was blessed with several tents full of children, but he chose—unwisely—to favor his son Joseph. You know the story of how Jacob documented this favoritism through the gift of a colorful coat (Gen 37:3). Joseph's dreams and an episode of a "bad report" against his brothers (Gen 37:2) combined with the favoritism to cause his brothers to hate him. After flirting with the idea of murder, they sold Joseph to slavers and faked his death (Gen 37:12–32). The plot was a partial success; Jacob wrongly concluded that Joseph was dead. As expected in that culture, "Then Jacob tore his garments and put sackcloth on his loins and mourned his son many days" (Gen 37:34). We appreciate the powerful reminder that different cultures, even subcultures, have unique grief rituals.

We don't think Joseph's brothers anticipated the extent of Jacob's grief. Despite their efforts at comfort, "He refused to be comforted and said, "No, I shall go down to Sheol to my son, mourning" (Gen 37:35). We grasp his meaning: "I'm going to grieve for the rest of my days. The loss of Joseph has become the defining moment of my life."

We assume his grief eventually stopped after he learned that Joseph was alive as a prince of Egypt (Gen 45:25–28). However, we acknowledge that it is just as feasible to assume that he traded one grief for another: "I have eight sons who knew the truth and would not tell me. I have eight sons who let me live for years in anguish."

Jacob's grief reminds us that even perceived loss leads to grief. It reminds us that grief can become life-defining. It reminds us that a person can refuse comfort and be trapped in life-long grief.

Hannah's grief was different. She grieved what she didn't have, a child with her husband, Elkanah (1 Sam 1). Elkanah made an effort to comfort her: "Hannah, why do you weep? And why do you not eat? And why is your heart so sad? Am I not more to you than ten sons?" (1 Sam 1:8) It didn't work. And her rival Peninah purposefully compounded her pain (1 Sam 1:6).

While we appreciate Elkanah's effort, it remains clumsy. He knew the source of her sadness. No matter how good he was to her, he could not fill the void in her heart. In this case, he unintentionally compounded the problem by choosing to have two wives. And we're left to wonder why there is no report of Elkanah joining Hannah in prayer for resolution.

Hannah's prayer for a son, spoken in grief, is one of the most moving in all of scripture (1 Sam 1:9ff). She took her pain to the Lord. She didn't lash out at the woman who afflicted her. She didn't redirect the pain of her grief to hatred of her husband. She unashamedly poured out her heart to God. All of this would have been just as faithful and proper even if the Lord had not blessed her with children. On top of that, her prayer of thanksgiving for deliverance is stunning (1 Sam 2:1–10)! It's even more stunning when we remember that she delighted in giving her son back to God rather than grieving her promise to do so.

David's grief for Absalom was both fierce and fiercely complicated. Absalom had murdered his brother (Amnon), conspired against his father the king, disgraced his father, and was attempting to take the kingdom by force (2 Sam 13:23–29, 15:1–6, 16:20–23). Despite all this, David still loved Absalom. His orders before the final battle are clear: "Deal gently for my sake with the young man Absalom" (2 Sam 18:5). Perhaps David remembers the part he played in this unfolding tragedy (2 Sam 12:7–12, 13:21). Certainly, he's practicing a denial, as there is no happy ending for a son who conspires, betrays, and kills. The sad legacy of sin, even sin that has been forgiven, often hounds people in unforeseen ways.

David's grief for Absalom is legendary: "O my son Absalom, my son, my son Absalom. Would I had died instead of you. O Absalom, my son, my son" (2 Sam 18:33). Many see both bitter pain and bargaining in these words. The words that follow in 2 Samuel 19 speak of depression. David covered his face and continued to repeat his lament. This part of the grief cycle was broken only after stout intervention by Joab, the king's ruthless general. We intend no disrespect, but if Joab is your grief counselor, you're in a world of hurt. With intervention, David moved to a degree of acceptance, and returned to Jerusalem.

David reminds us that it's possible to grieve a loss as it is unfolding, even before it is finalized. We often see this in cases of terminal illness. Once the death comes, observers are surprised that there are no tears and that there is what appears to be relatively quick acceptance. In reality, the river of tears was cried during the dying process and what people see as "the loss" was actually the last small step in a series of fierce losses. If you searched the literature, you'd find this described as anticipatory grief. We're so wise not to be shocked. We're even wiser not to judge.

David reminds us that some grief is infinitely complicated. The more difficult one's relationship, the more challenging the grief. It's like working on a black jigsaw puzzle in a dark room while blindfolded and wearing thick gloves. Even those who know God struggle mightily. We don't understand how those who don't know God cope (2 Cor 1:3–4; 1 Pet 5:6–7). As difficult as it is, we dare not abandon people in such times.

Jeremiah is rightly known as the weeping prophet. Other than David, he teaches us more about lament than anyone save Jesus (Matt 23:37–39). Jeremiah watched his nation self-destruct and God's subsequent judgment through a series of Babylonian invasions. By revelation, he knew he was living a "Greek tragedy" (Jer 1:10–2:37, 5:14–17). No matter what he did, the die had been cast. Individuals would be preserved and protected, but the nation was doomed (Jer 5:18–19).

Jeremiah documents the power of lament. Crying people make us uncomfortable. We want to comfort; we prefer to help bring immediate relief. Sometimes there is no relief, at least not in the form or to the degree that we want it. Sometimes the loss is coming no matter what we do. Stopping the loss isn't an option. But staying with God and letting Him help us are always sound options.

The book of Lamentations is written for the grieving —and for all who need to prepare to grieve. The nation was like a widow, like a princess who had fallen into slavery (Lam 1:1). Bitter weeping flowed from bad memories and loss (Lam 1:2). There was no rest and no relief (Lam 1:3, 1:7). They faced unanswerable questions (Lam 2:11–13). It seemed that God has permanently forsaken (Lam 2:17–19).

Jeremiah makes clear that it's permissible to state our pains, our doubts, our fears, our struggles, and our confusion (Lam 3:1–18). Such expression often leads to reflection and self-examination. Such expression often leads to humility, trust in God, and holy dependence. It helps us learn just how much we need God. Even in the face of unspeakable trial, we realize that God remains—and so do we. That's Lamentations 3:22-24, "The steadfast love of the Lord never ceases, His mercies never come to an end, they are new every morning, great is Your faithfulness. 'The Lord is my portion' says my soul, therefore I will hope in Him." The goodness of God will return, in God's due time, to those who wait for Him (Lam 3:25-27). Wait on the Lord, don't surrender hope, and hold on to faith. Deliverance will come (Lam 3:31-33).

Yes, this is a somewhat poetic reading of Lamentations. Jeremiah spoke specifically to a sinful nation reaping havoc for generations of sin. Certainly, we aren't asserting that all personal grief flows directly from sin. We also don't claim that the bottom line of Lamentations is a spiritual version of "Take your medicine. You earned this. After a time, everything will be okay, just as it was before." We're on a different level. The principles taught in Lamentations stand as long as earth stands. In times of great loss, we're blessed to talk to God. No one hears like God hears. In times of great pain, lean on God. Learn the lessons that can be learned, but endure even when major questions go unanswered. Whether in this life or the next, God sustains, heals, and delivers. "In Him we live and move and have our being" (Acts 17:28). It's right—and we're blessed—to hope in Him. It's right—and we're blessed—to help others rediscover their hope in God.

HOW CAN CHURCH LEADERS HELP THE GRIEVING?

Show up. As a rule, we do well immediately after a loss, particularly a death. We bring food, we send flowers, and we attend the visitation. Then, as a rule, we disappear. With grieving, after care is so important. It's also challenging. Grieving people will often tell us, "I'm fine. I don't need a babysitter. I prefer to be alone." Often, that's the depression talking. Keep showing up.

Back to the first rule of counseling: Do no harm. Don't make it worse. We can help by unlearning false information and rejecting false assumptions about grief. There's no shame in ignorance on any subject, but there's great shame in both willful and ongoing ignorance. It's powerful to know something of what we don't know.

We can share information that helps grieving people understand at least some aspects of what's happening to them. "No, you are not crazy. Grief makes many feel what you're now feeling and think what you're now thinking." "You won't always feel as bad as you feel right now. We weren't made to live permanently at this level of pain." "There is no clock or calendar. This process will take the time that it takes. Please don't let anyone put you on some imaginary schedule." "You've experienced major loss. Life will be different moving forward. You will find yourself in a new reality with a new normal." "You are not in this alone. God is with you and so are we."

We can listen. Please remember chapter 5 on the basics of listening. One of life's most foolish statements is, "I felt so helpless. All I could do was listen." There's tremendous power in opening our hearts and giving our time to hear others—especially those who are hurting. A reminder: The grieving often need to repeat both facts and stories. Please let them. It's one of the ways they cope and stabilize. It's one of the ways they keep themselves sane.

When the time is right, offer gentle encouragement. Reject any idea of pushing or demanding progress. Seek ways to pull them toward God, faith, and life. Invite healing, speak with realistic optimism, and lend hope. Hoping for people before they can hope for themselves is one of life's sacred works.

In due time and if essential, gently challenge errant thinking and dysfunctional behaviors. This is not a Week One recommendation. It's almost never a Month One recommendation. The deeper the loss, the more time we'll allow. Grieving is very seldom like being thrown from a horse, where "the quicker you get back on, the better."

"Pray without ceasing" (1 Thess 5:17). Pre-pray, pray, and re-pray. Then, pray more. Pray for wisdom (Jas 1:5). Pray for patience. Pray for perseverance. Pray for healing. Pray for comfort.

THREE MISTAKES TO AVOID

Particularly with grief due to death, some people suggest, "Never speak the name of the deceased. It's rude and harmful to stir painful memories." Not all memories are painful. Speaking the names of good people helps keep good memories alive. Speaking the names of Christians reminds family that they continue to live with Jesus "in God's tomorrow." The foolishness of this suggestion under most circumstances lies in its assumption that the major loss of a loved one isn't remembered by the grieving every moment of every day.

With every form of grieving, some have a decided need to fix things, to make everything right. Trying to fix the unfixable is folly of the highest order. By definition, it can't be done. Such attempts to meet impossible standards frustrate everyone. Those attempts also waste resources and opportunities that could be profitably employed.

Please avoid falling into clichés. Arguably the worst is, "I know just how you feel." Given the jet wash of major grief, an honest griever might respond, "Great. Please tell me, because I sure don't know." "Which millisecond are you talking about? In the last two seconds, I've felt angry, frustrated, hopeless, lost, sad, forsaken, blessed, comforted, loved, and destroyed. Tell me, which of those am I feeling right now?"

Additional clichés include "You'll feel better soon." ("Soon" is difficult to define and seldom soon enough.) "This too shall pass." "Loss comes to everyone." "Grief is a natural part of life." Each of these truisms offers little comfort and carries high risk of being perceived as an insult. None meet the standard of "a word fitly spoken" (Prov 25:11) or speech that is "gracious, seasoned with salt" (Col 4:6).

Perhaps I shouldn't share one of the games played by parts of my family at funeral homes as we receive those who come to pay their respects. We call it The Dumbest Thing. At the end of the evening we compare answers to

"What's the dumbest thing you heard anyone say tonight?" We limited ourselves to things said in attempts to be comforting. After we laugh and cringe, we try to be forgiving. Then, we promise ourselves to avoid all such foolish words.

ENDNOTE

[1.] Elizabeth Kubler-Ross, *On Death and Dying: What the Dying Have to Teach Doctors, Nurses, Clergy, and Their Own Families* (New York: Simon & Schuster, 1969).

CHAPTER 14
HELPING THE UNDER-
CONNECTED

Few would question the assertion that people need social and emotional connection. In the iconic movie, Tom Hanks battled loneliness by "inventing" a friend; he created Wilson by painting a face on a volleyball. Prisoners who misbehave are moved to solitary confinement. Extreme isolation is viewed as a form of torture. In church we sometimes sing, "But I don't know a thing in this whole wide world that's worse than being alone." That idea is more commonly worded, "There's nothing worse than being alone." Various sages slightly disagree, one stating, "There is something worse than being alone. It's being with a person who makes you feel alone." Another adds, "There's nothing worse than being alone in a crowd." We've even heard tearful people say, "I feel so alone in my family." Loneliness and related issues are emotive, pervasive, discouraging, and complex.

Biblically speaking, all was good in creation until "The Lord God said, 'It is not good that the man should be alone'" (Gen 2:18). David appealed to God, "Turn to me and be gracious to me, for I am lonely and afflicted" (Ps 25:16). In times of persecution, he described himself poetically: "I am like a desert owl in the wilderness, like an owl in the waste places. I lie awake; I am like a lonely sparrow on the housetop" (Ps 102:6–7). At the depth of his depression, Elijah lamented his aloneness (1 Kgs 19:10). On the night of His betrayal, Jesus didn't want to be alone in His prayers (Matt 26:37–38). Paul lamented being forsaken and alone (at least from a human perspective) at times during his Roman imprisonment (2 Tim 4:9–16).

There are degrees of under-connectedness. In the extreme, people feel totally alone—unloved, unneeded, unwanted, unimportant, not cared for, and not valued. More moderate, but still painful versions include feeling under-loved, under-appreciated, and under-valued. Google "loneliness" and you'll get millions of hits, including descriptions of an epidemic of loneliness with fierce health, social, and emotional costs. Few seem to have all the friends they want. Even fewer have both the number and depth of quality relationships that they desire.

UNDER-CONNECTION IN A CHURCH SETTING

Whether no friendships, few friendships, or shallow friendships, under-connectedness poses extra challenges for Christians. We see Jesus and His disciples purposefully together. "And He appointed twelve (whom He named apostles) so that they might be with Him" (Mark 3:14). After the resurrection, we find the apostles waiting in Jerusalem as part of a group of about 120 believers: "All these with one accord were devoting themselves to prayer (Acts 1:14). Acts 2:41–47 beautifully describes the devotion, closeness, fellowship, and love of the first Christians. Similar descriptions abound (Acts 4:32, 6:1–7, 20:36–38; Rom 1:8–13; Eph 2:19–22, 4:32; 1 Thess 4:9–10). Other passages enjoin love, care, closeness, and unity (Rom 12:9–13; 1 Cor 1:10, 12:26–27; Phil 2:1–4; Col 3:12–17; Heb 13:1–3; 1 Pet 2:17, 4:8–10). We know love for one another is a key and essential characteristic of God's family (John 13:34–35; 1 John 3–4).

Bluntly, we know how life in God's church is supposed to be. It's to be permeated by ever-growing love, respect, and fellowship. Christians can't ignore or neglect other Christians. We're the kingdom of right relationships. We have God's example in reconciliation, forgiveness, and sacrificial service. We know better than to let people suffer or struggle alone.

CAVEATS: REASONS FOR UNDER-CONNECTEDNESS

To be fair, it isn't always the fault of the church when fellow Christians are lonely. Some resist healthy connections. The classic example remains the person who arrives five minutes late for worship, leaves five minutes early, and then complains, "No one spoke to me." Some choose this approach because it's an effective mechanism for distancing.

Why would a person choose distancing? There are many reasons, including guilt over ongoing sin, shame/embarrassment, lack of social skills and the accompanying fear of failure in relationship development, and unbiblical assumptions learned within dysfunctional families. Among those assumptions are *"I'm not worthy of friendship/love," "No one would want my friendship," "Since I have Jesus, I don't need others," "My physical family is all I need," "Everybody already has all the friends that they need,"* and *"I have nothing to offer others."* Regrettably, some parents and spouses teach these falsehoods. And some teach these lies to themselves.

Others choose to keep their distance because they have made strong effort in the past only to be rejected, harmed, or otherwise disappointed. Harm includes both dashed expectations and the creation of smothering, controlling, or otherwise abusive relationships. On the other hand, it can be as simple as hyper-awareness of societal mobility. *"Why bother to make close friends? Either they'll move or I will. It's just not worth the effort."* We've even heard people say, *"I don't make friends. That way I won't have to be sad when they die."*

We mention these factors to invite church leaders to listen well and love fiercely. Pain is a tough teacher. People who have been hurt don't want a repeat performance. Self-protection is a powerful instinct, so powerful that it often causes people to harm themselves as part of their effort at self-protection. It's like never learning to swim because I almost drowned as a child or never learning to drive because my parents once had a wreck.

If we can find a way to spend time with those who appear lonely or distant, they will either tell or show us why. Knowing the reason isn't a matter of curiosity. The more we know, the better we're able to tailor and target our attempts to help. Suppose we never learn? Sometimes caring enough to try and knowing not to push/demand will open the doors of progress and opportunity. While it's sometimes helpful, it's not always essential that we know the source of the struggle.

Sometimes the church contributes to under-connectedness. In what ways? A classic example is by segmenting various ministries so strictly that we inhibit the opportunity for the development of intergenerational friendships. The Bible gives strong emphasis to the benefits and blessings of older believers blessing the younger (Gen 18:17–19; Deut 6:1–9; 2 Tim 1:3–5; Titus 2:1–8). It also acknowledges that the younger can bless and encourage the older (1 Tim 4:12–16; Titus 2:6–8). The healthy opposite of over-segmenting is mentoring programs that encourage older members to partner with the younger and adopt-a-grandparent ministries that encourage younger believers to treat older members as family.

A second way congregations unintentionally contribute to under-connectedness is by planning activities that are structured toward extroverts. We love to see churches purposefully include opportunities where those who are more reserved get to share their lives and talents. Some need smaller and quieter venues to tell their stories of faith and growth.

Some churches still plan activities primarily for nuclear families—mom, dad, and the kids. While we love that biblical family model, we know that from a statistical perspective it is no longer the predominant model in our culture. From single parent families to couples with no children to couples with no children at home to single-member families, families come in all shapes, forms, and sizes. We don't want the underconnected to feel "planned around" or excluded.

HOW DO WE HELP THE UNDERCONNECTED?

Please avoid reading this section as a checklist. Consider it globally. Think of it as part worldview, part commitment, a partial list of techniques, and an invitation to creativity.

Be nice (Prov 18:24). Be nice to the nice, the non-nice, the enigmatic, and even the mean. Live graciously. Talk graciously. Speak to people. Fiercely and consistently practice the Golden Rule (Matt 5:43-48 & 7:12; Rom 12:14-21; Gal 6:10). Treat people better than they deserve. Treat people better than you have to.

Remember the power of small things. On a rough day, simple acknowledgment can be a treasure. A word of encouragement—whether gratitude or compliment—has remarkable power (Prov 25:11-12 & 25). There's no substitute for sincerity or specificity in offering praise.

Among the most powerful "small things" are small changes and small efforts. We can invite the underconnected to try a small outreach to a potential friend. If it succeeds at any level, use the energy from that success to take the next step. If it doesn't succeed, praise the effort and the courage to try. Process what happened. What can be learned for next time? What could be tweaked? If there's enough trust to allow, consider asking, "Is it possible that you tried too hard?" If that can be discussed, we get a major teaching opportunity. Few aspects of human relationships work better under pressure. Outside boot camp and some athletic teams, virtually everything works better within the ebb and flow of life.

Flowing from the section above, create a safe environment for listening. To quote a wise friend, "Trust the process." Be willing to wait for each person to tell his or her story. If the story includes pain and disappointment with people, become an instrument of healing through loving listening. It is possible for some people to "talk the pain out"—at least to some degree. Some achieve a degree of self-awareness and self-understanding as they "speak their pain." For some, being able to name and describe the pain creates a space for healing.

Even if the pain story is factually ridiculous, don't judge or condemn. Listen, learn, and use what you learn to promote healing and growth. Pain is never ridiculous to the person it's plaguing.

To use the least technical jargon, listen for and gently challenge stinkin' thinkin'. Suppose an under-connected person's assumption is, *"I can't build quality relationships because I've tried in the past and failed."* These are examples of the kind of questions that we might ask:

- Can you tell me about the effort that you made?
- In what context was that effort made? Might your current context be better/stronger in any ways?
- What skills do you have now that you didn't have then?

- What have you learned about life that you didn't know then?
- If you could have a "do over," what would you do differently—more wisely—knowing what you know now? Did you frighten your potential friend by trying too hard? Did you expect too much too soon? Did you give things time to develop?

If an under-connected individual says or implies, "I'm not worthy of having friends and being loved," remember the power of Scripture. There's something wonderful about reminding people that we're all made in the image of God and loved by God (Gen 1:26–27; John 3:16). Experience and common sense will help here. It may be that some need to hear a statement of rebuttal: "I'm sorry, but I must disagree. God does love you." Others will find greater benefit in a question: "You do know that God loves you, don't you?"

Maybe the opposite assumption or comment is made: "I know I'm under-connected at the moment. I need and want a best friend forever. But I'm waiting for the perfect friend. I have an image of that person in my heart, and I'll know her (or him) as soon as I see her." There's much to unpack in that statement. There's an assumption that each of us gets just one best friend for life. Reality suggests that we may have various best friends at various stages of life. There's an assumption that "a perfect best friend" exists. People don't come in "perfects." "Perfect" is an impossible standard to set for anyone. While there's nothing wrong with dreaming of and describing the kind of best friend we want, the extreme form of that dream forgets that most friendships develop. They don't begin at maximum joy, strength, and benefit. They grow.

A caveat is in order. While we know no person is perfect, we don't want to encourage those whom we're helping to settle for friendships that don't bless. There are "friendships" that cause more harm than good. There are "friends" whom we don't need (Prov 22:24–25, 1 Cor 15:33, Jas 4:4). When seeking godly relationships, admire and appreciate high standards so long as those standards fall within the bounds of reason. There's protection in setting high standards, but there's no blessing in unattainable expectations.

You know what we're recommending here. Listen and learn. Don't assume a judgmental or hyper-critical stance. Be careful of assumptions. At the same time, formulate hypotheses. Listen for themes. Note dangerous assumptions. Look for thoughts and behaviors that may be sabotaging the development of godly, lasting friendships.

If the person's assumption is, "Nobody would want my friendship" or "No one would benefit from being my friend," a bit of bewilderment might be in order as we respond with something similar to "I don't mean to be rude, but how could you know that?" Sometimes, we can "say" that with our faces or hands without needing the words. If the person is on any level already our friend, we have extra advantage. We can kindly and gently disagree in the moment. "Sorry, I don't mean to be rude, but I find our friendship to be a blessing." Warning: if we say this, be prepared to give at least a few reasons or examples. We are likely to be asked.

What if the assumption is, "People are so mobile these days. Why go to the trouble of making close friends only to have them move away?" Most of us have friends who remain emotionally close even though they're physically distant. Due to mission work, we have friends on other continents. From WhatsApp to FaceTime, communicating is cheaper, more convenient, and more personal than ever. Don't fear kindly challenging bad thinking. The ripple effect of errant thinking is too strong and too damaging to let it stand. Bad thinking always manifests in pain and loss.

Some may suffer from overarching unrealistic expectations of friendship. One of the more common is "I must find the one friend who will make me happy." While healthy relationships contribute heavily to the joy and quality of life, there's a fundamental flaw in asserting that another person has the power to "make me happy." If it were true, it would be fearsome. Could it ever be wise to grant another flawed human that much power?

There's a second MAJOR concern with "I must find the one friend who will make me happy." That statement flows from the perspective of being served rather than serving. Its viewpoint is the very opposite of Jesus's words from Matthew 20:28. We have seen people choose to abandon the selfish perspective in favor of the serving view. They stopped looking for the perfect friend and began trying to be a better friend to others. It's one of life's more remarkable changes. It's also a remarkable paradox. When we serve others, God helps us build the loving relationships that we need.

There's also an unrealistic expectation that we call the Myth of Exclusivity: "If my friend has other friends, then he/she doesn't really care for me." This assertion flows from errant zero-sum thinking. It assumes that love and good will are finite commodities—any concern you show to others reduces the amount of concern available for me. Mature people know love doesn't work that way. Time is finite, but love isn't. People aren't limited to one friend at a time. Attempting to hoard a friend always ends in frustration.

Logically, the Myth of Exclusivity limits each of us to one friend. We know by observation that isn't the norm. People tend to have work friends, church friends, online friends, and more. But to be fair, we should acknowledge that "there are friends, and then there are FRIENDS." There's the beautiful language of 1 Samuel 18:1: "the soul of Jonathan was knit to the soul of David." It continues in the loving lament of 2 Samuel 1:25–26. After nearly 3,000 years, we are still moved by Ruth's devotion to Naomi (Ruth 1:16–17). We appreciate how the Apostle John sweetly referred to himself as "the disciple whom Jesus loved" (John 21:20). There's no sin and no flaw in the fact that some relationships are stunningly closer than others.

SPIRITUAL PATHS TO MAKING CONNECTIONS

As we encourage others to build the friendships they desire, three obvious truths merit mention.

For people with spiritual inclination, there's something stunningly attractive about Jesus (Matt 7:28–29, Mark 12:37). As we add the fruit of the Spirit and the Christian virtues, we become more attractive and inviting to those who love Jesus (Gal 5:22–25, 2 Pet 1:5–11). Becoming more like Jesus is a time-honored path to loving, lasting relationships.

Biblical scholars love to remind us that the Greek word for fellowship, *koinonia*, fundamentally means "joint participation." Doing God's work together is another time-honored path to close, caring relationships (Acts 2:46–47, Rom 16:24, 1 Cor 16:13–18, Phil 2:25–30 & 4:10–19). As we work together to honor God, the very best relationships form and deepen.

While we value every godly relationship, we don't even pretend that the one with the most friends wins. Wins what? There is no contest or competition. When it comes to brotherhood, friendship, and camaraderie, we know to value quality over quantity. There are few blessings greater than having a great friend. There are few treasures more precious than being one.

CHAPTER 15
HELPING PEOPLE UNSTICK

Sometimes the stuck know that they're stuck, and that's a blessing. "I was reading Ephesians 4:11–16. I realize that I'm not where I need to be. I don't have the 'mature manhood' that 'the knowledge of the Son of God' brings. I'm nowhere near 'the measure of the stature of the fullness of Christ.'" Those hurting souls will seek the help of those they consider church leaders. They'll speak their pain and their hope: "I want 'to grow up in every way into Him who is the head, into Christ.' I'm stuck in my spiritual life and I need your help." People can reach the same conclusion from 1 Corinthians 13, Galatians 5:22–26, or 2 Peter 1:5–11. Thank God for such humble and honest folks!

More often, the spiritually stuck don't have those insights. They know they don't feel right, they know "there has to be more" or "there has to be better," but they don't know how or why. In the saddest cases, they feel that they are being held back by others. They can't tell you how or why, but they know things aren't right, and they're certain it's not their fault. And those are among the hardest cases. What could be more challenging? Think of those who have no awareness of their malaise and/or no desire to be any better than they are right now.

Decades ago, my (Bill's) dad served on the county school board. One of his greatest insights from that tenure came from a state-sponsored developmental session. It discussed the most challenging of students, those who "didn't need no education, didn't want no education," and were resisting education with all their might. And the presenter said to the board members, "And it's your responsibility to offer them education."

In the worst of cases, working with "the stuck" reminds us of God's word to Jeremiah: "They will fight against you" (Jer 1:19). This proved painfully accurate, "As for the word that you have spoken to us in the name of the Lord, we will not listen to you" (Jer 44:16). Ezekiel 3:6–7 is just as applicable, particularly: "The house of Israel will not be willing to listen to you."

Our purpose is not to discourage, but to steel the resolve of faithful church leaders who must live up to God's commission. Three initial implications are clear. First, not all the stuck are alike. They differ in insight, attitude, and willingness. Disaster follows if we make the mistake of lumping them all into one group.

Second, love demands that we help those who need us. We offer help even when people don't yet know that it's needed. We offer help even when it isn't wanted. This will require faith, love, courage, and creativity.

Third, we offer help while maintaining realistic expectations. Like all of God's leaders, we won't always see the results for which we pray. People can stay stuck even if it hurts them. Even sadder, people can stay stuck even if it kills them. Sometimes it does (Rev 3:16).

CAVEATS

This chapter will speak of the "spiritually stuck," those whose spiritual growth has stopped. More broadly, it will also address those who either feel or actually are "stuck" more generally. Some feel stuck in dysfunctional or less-than-they-could-be relationships: "I could be more for God if only I wasn't stuck in this marriage. Everything would be different if I had a partner who helped me." Some feel stuck in their level of church involvement, in the shallowness or narrowness of their service to God: "I want to do more in the kingdom, but there's no way I can right now." Others feel emotionally and/or intellectually stuck. They want broader, deeper, more fulfilling lives, but they don't know how to move forward: "I don't know what to do next. Seems like every time I try to improve, things backfire. It just never works." As you may already know, these categories are not mutually exclusive. Fortunately, there is no category of human need that God's word fails to address at least on the level of principle.

HELPING THOSE WHO REQUEST OUR HELP

Often those who know they're stuck and seek help already possess numerous answers and options. When they seek our counsel, their primary need may be validation: "I need to check my thinking. Am I seeing this clearly? Am I on the right track? Is there something BIG that I'm missing?"

There's joy in working with such people. It's low pressure and low risk. We listen, listen, and listen more. We affirm all that's good and godly. We show support and love. In the best of situations, we say next to nothing, and they thank us profusely for being so helpful. And we give God the glory.

Sometimes the need is greater than offering validation and serving as a sounding board. Not to be flippant, but sometimes our role is cheerleader and motivator. Good people can know what they need to do, but struggle to find the energy and impetus to start. Think of Gideon in Judges 6:12. God's call through the angel is, "The Lord is with you, O mighty man of valor!" Admittedly, God reached out to Gideon, but our point turns on how God reached out. God called Gideon not what he was—an oppressed man threshing wheat in a winepress, but what he would become—a deliverer, a man of God, a mighty man of valor.

Through the angel, God lent hope to Gideon. God infused Gideon with a dream. As the story unfolded, God gave Gideon signs of His presence, small successes along the way, reinforcement of faith, and ultimate victory. We can do the same for those who seek our help.

The devil would love to have us believe that cheerleading is beneath us. You know the approach. "As you try to help people, keep both feet on the ground. Some will do well, but many won't. Don't inflate your expectations. Don't try too hard. Either they will or they won't change. The ultimate decision isn't yours." The best lies include as much truth as is possible. Keep both feet on the ground, but hope for and with others. Lend your wholehearted support to every effort to do God's work and draw closer to Him. Don't seem indifferent. We don't leave people to sink or swim when it's within our ability to assist.

When people seek our assistance to grow, we listen to their ideas, and we support all that's good. Then, we offer helpful tweaks and additional ideas for consideration. Often those come in the form of "I love your idea! Have you thought about adding ____ or asking ____ to partner with you?" The goal is never to take over their thinking. Rather, we ally with and invite them to enhance their own good ideas. In this regard, we're somewhat like David with the temple. David proposed building a temple for the Lord but was not allowed to do so (2 Sam 7). Rather than pout or attempt to circumvent the Lord's will, David began collecting material to make the eventual construction easier for his son. We love the principle: Do what you can that's right to help every good work.

What of those who know they're stuck but haven't yet discovered answers, or who don't yet see a path forward? We recommend beginning with a series of compliments. "God bless you for your courage. God bless you for wanting to be more and do more in His service. That's a great beginning." "Thank you for your obvious desire to grow. It's amazing to think of what God can do with such desire."

Follow the compliments with exploration. "Obviously, you want to grow. Could you tell me what you've tried so far and how that's worked out?" Explore not only what has been attempted, but also how and under what conditions the attempts were made. Their concept might have been brilliant, but the execution poor. Sometimes all that's needed is a tweak. They might have tried before or tried without prayer. The need might be to appeal for God's blessing and guidance first. They might have tried alone when the concept is workable only as a team effort. Bottom line: Don't dismiss ideas without evaluation.

If their insight is so new that they can't list actions they've taken, change the question to "Can you tell me what you've thought about trying?" Some benefit from brainstorming. Others will need your help to start the process. It's not uncommon to hear, "I really have no clue. I just know that I want to do better. I want to be more like Jesus. I want to be a better servant, but I don't know how." Those statements deserve their own set of compliments. They also merit a substantive response.

A key principle when helping stuck people is to never underestimate the power of small changes. If we're stuck at Level A and our goal is Level Z, many of us fail to remember B through Y. The chasm from A to Z is often too large to leap. Instead of thinking of one huge leap, we help people think of building essential bridges. These bridges are built one span at a time.

When considering the power of small changes, the first great insight is helping people differentiate what they can change and what they can't. The easiest example? We can change much about ourselves, but we do not have the power to change others. Admittedly, as we improve, we invite and encourage those around us to grow as well, but we can't make them grow. Choose to change something that's relevant and changeable.

Use the power and victory of that small change as energy and motivation for the next small change. Expect setbacks and opposition. Know that zig-zag is likely. Think of God's long-term development plan for Moses —forty years in Egypt, forty years in the wilderness, then forty years of leadership. Think of Peter's growth as he learned from Jesus. Even John didn't start his ministry as the disciple of love. Growth is often two steps forward and one step back. Focus on the direction, the positive movement. For Christians, Galatians 6:9 is always in play: "And let us not grow weary in doing good, for in due season we will reap, if we do not give up."

One of our favorite aspects of helping those who seek help, accept help, and grow to God's glory is reminding people to celebrate every victory that God gives. As church leaders, people will appreciate that we notice their progress. It's a great opportunity for encouragement. It's the perfect positive aspect of "if you see something, say something." The word might need to be quiet and measured; one of our favorite lines is, "Catch somebody doing good and say so." Jesus did this often (Matt 8:10–13, 9:2 & 22, 15:28, 16:17). Don't accept the false notion that celebrating incremental victories is beneath us or indicates that we've settled for less than God's best.

HELPING THE STUCK WHO DON'T KNOW THEY'RE STUCK

We may best approach this section by thinking in categories. Some suffer from general malaise. They live like robots, following the programming but not knowing why. On some level, they know there's more, but they have no clue what "more" is, what it looks like, whether it's worth seeking, or whether it's attainable.

Vibrant living begins with Genesis 1:26–27; we are made in God's image. Vibrant living chooses to believe Psalm 8; we're made "a little lower than the heavenly beings" and "crowned with glory and honor." God seeks our worship (John 4:23–24). God has shown—and continues to demonstrate—His love for us (Rom 5:6–11). Jesus came to save, reconcile, and offer abundant life (John 1:11–13, 3:16–17, 10:10, & 14:1–4). Jesus makes our lives and sacrifices acceptable to the Father (Rom 12:1–2, Phil 4:18, 1 Pet 2:5). In Christ, we are able to bless one another (Rom 12:3–13). In Christ we are empowered to bring glory to God (Matt 5:16, 1 Pet 2:11–12).

In Christ, there is purpose and nobility in even the smallest acts of service. Think of one who gives "even a cup of cold water because he is a disciple" (Matt 10:42). Consider the lady who anointed Jesus as per Mark 14:3–9: "[W]herever the gospel is proclaimed in the whole world, what she has done will be told in memory of her." Remember the widow's two small coins (Mark 12:42). Think of Dorcas (Acts 9:36–43). Remember the unspecified service of Phoebe (Rom 16:1–2) and Philemon, who refreshed "the souls of the saints (Phlm 7).

To get unstuck in terms of growth and service, we do the good we know to do, no matter how small. We find someone who needs help and act. To quote the phrase from the ad, "Just do it!" No service is small to the grateful heart. No service that honors God can ever be deemed small.

Practically, it's easier to do good with a partner.

When Jesus sent the disciples to preach and do good, He sent them two-by-two (Mark 6:7). The Spirit called the first missionaries as a team (Acts 11). Paul kept adding to the mission team. There's great power in helping people make serving connections. Of course, none of us is limited to a single partner in service. Our hope is that some of these partnerships will expand beyond the dyad and that a web effect will follow.

There can also be power in sharing stories of personal growth, particularly stories of getting unstuck. Our personal stories are not normative; they never hold the power of scripture. However, they can be motivational when shared in the appropriate time and manner (Prov 25:11–12, Acts 22:1–21).

For some suffering from general malaise, there will be benefit in exploring the reason they became stuck. How will we know whether this is the case? There's a rule in people helping that says, "The past matters only when it matters." If it matters to the person whom you're helping, then it matters. If not, exploring causation may be a waste of time. Knowing the cause of a problem is not always essential to its cure. To offer the simplest example, it's not essential to know how and when the splinter entered my finger. I just need to remove it, treat the wound, and move on.

One of the most frustrating categories of "stuck people" is those who are stuck and suffering but have pronounced themselves helpless victims. Often, they have constructed a "stuckness narrative": "I know the moment when I lost my spark and confidence. I shared my plan for great ministry with ___ and they shot it down. I've never been the same since." For some, this story may be true—factual. They had a good plan, it was shot down, and they let that episode become life defining. However, such stories are never true spiritually. How do we know?

Consider Jacob and Joseph. Jacob lived years stuck in grief for Joseph, thinking he was dead (Gen 37:35). Even through mountainous setbacks (being sold as a slave, being falsely accused and imprisoned, being forgotten in prison), Joseph's life is the very opposite of "stuckness." Remember Joshua and Caleb. They were defeated in the moment by the ten faithless spies (Num 13). Their entry into Canaan was delayed by forty years. Yet neither of them lost faith. Both stand as outstanding examples (Josh 14:6–15, 24:1–31). The same is true of Paul. He so wanted to visit the saints in Rome, but was prevented for years. Yet, he did not become stuck (Rom 1:8–15). Paul had dreams of preaching in Asia and Bithynia but was forbidden by the Spirit to do so (Acts 16:6–7). But he took the next open door that God provided.

What happens to us doesn't define us. We are defined by how we respond to life's victories and trials. God always offers a path forward (Rom 8:31–39). That said, we make no claim that God's path is pain-free.

Whatever happens, there is no blessing in holding on to blame and victimhood. God will avenge the wrongs done to us (Rom 12:11–21). That frees us to move forward with God through grace. Blame and victimhood are glue and cement that cruelly imprison.

STUCK PEOPLE WHO DO NOT WANT TO CHANGE

Another challenging category of "stuck people" is those who do not want to change. "Stuckness" has become part of their identity, their comfort zone. Sometimes we hear it in these words: "I've been like I am for so long, there's no use changing now. Probably couldn't change even if I tried. Not sure I want to try."

There is no formula for overcoming such thinking. The thinking isn't accurate; it leaves God out of the equation (Ezek 37). What do we recommend to church leaders who encounter it? Plant a seed of faith. Remind the person that God has done and continues to do things that are impossible for mere humans (Matt 19:26). Pray (Luke 18:1, 1 Thess 5:17). Wait for the next major life event. It's amazing how life events can open doors to change and growth—the birth of a baby (child or grandchild), a health change, a job change, a move, or the death of someone close. Be there with love and a word from the Lord when those life events come. Speak of hope. Share something of the goodness of the Lord. And be thankfully amazed when God surprises us all —AGAIN.

CHAPTER 16

HELPING PEOPLE UPGRADE
THEIR HABITS

"Habits"[1] is a broad, flexible, and often confusing word. At the negative extreme, some associate it with addictions like tobacco use or excessive texting. At the hyper-positive, some assert that virtually all of life's challenges can be overcome by ingraining excellent habits. Of course there's huge territory between these extremes. Some see habits as mindless—and sometimes they are robotic. Others view them "life hacks" that simplify routine tasks and maximize resource availability (brain power, energy, and time) for more important matters. On the highest level, good habits are carefully chosen and honed patterns of thought and behavior that help us live our values more consistently and efficiently.

There are good, bad, and neutral habits. We know the wisdom of brushing our teeth, wearing our seatbelts, and looking both ways before we cross the street. We know something of the harm of grinding our teeth, being consistently late, or using insulting language ("That's stupid," "You idiot," or "Oh, my God"). On our better days, we smile at habits that we classify as quirks—twirling one's hair, cracking one's knuckles, or frequently using a harmless pet phrase ("Now, how about that?" "Oh my," or "Isn't that something?").

WHY SHOULD WE CARE ABOUT HABITS?

Good habits make us better. We still remember being taught, "As Abraham journeyed with God, you could trace his travels by the altars that he built" (Gen 12:7–8, 13:4 & 18). We make no suggestion that Abraham did this merely out of habit; there's no reason to question his devotion to God. We'd say the same about Job's prayer and sacrifice for his children, which "Job did continually" (Job 1:5). Elkanah acted similarly, going up "year by year from his city to worship and to sacrifice to the Lord of hosts at Shiloh" (1 Sam 1:4). The exemplary woman of Proverbs 31 embodied habits of trustworthiness, a strong work ethic, concern for others, kind communication, vigilance, and respect for God. Daniel passionately practiced a most impressive habit of prayer (Dan 2:17–18, 6:10, 9:3–27).

We see faithful spiritual habits in the life of Jesus: "And He came to Nazareth, where He had been brought up. And as was His custom, He went to the synagogue on the Sabbath day, and He stood up to read" (Luke 4:16). We also read the story of Jesus's early morning prayer as anything but a one-of-a-kind report (Mark 1:35). The aged prophetess Anna is praised for her continual "worshiping with fasting and prayer" (Luke 2:37).

Paul was known for his consistent habit of praying

for the brethren (Rom 1:8–12, 1 Cor 1:4–9, 2 Cor 11:28–29, Eph 1:15–23, Phil 1:3–7, Col 1:3–8, 1 Thess 1:2–4). Even before he was a Christian, Cornelius "prayed continually to God" (Acts 10:2). It makes sense that his generous almsgiving was also a habitual spiritual practice. Paul praised Stephanas and his family who "devoted themselves to the service of the saints" (1 Cor 16:15). Paul recommended strong habits of study and discipline to Timothy (1 Tim 4:12–16). Titus was commissioned to encourage brethren to practice a habit of good works (Titus 1:16; 2:7 & 14; 3:1, 8, & 14).

Bad habits can harm our health, character, influence, relationships, and spiritual service. "Habit" is not a frequent word in standard translations of the Bible. Within the English Standard Version, only Hebrews 10:25 speaks to this point: "not neglecting to meet together, as is the habit of some." There are, however, numerous warnings of the danger of bad habits. According to one of their own prophets, "Cretans are always liars, evil beasts, lazy gluttons" (Titus 1:12). We're suggesting that their poor reputation flowed from their habitual behavior. Titus 3:9–11 strongly suggests that some in Crete had a destructive habit of being quarrelsome, contentious, and divisive. 1 Timothy 6:3–5 suggests that this attitude also existed in Ephesus.

If we think of laziness as a habit, the Proverbs staunchly oppose it (Prov 6:6–11, 10:4–5 & 23, 12:27, 13:4, 15:19, 16:24, 18:9, 19:24, 20:4, 22:13, 24:30–34, 26:13–16). They also oppose the habits of disdaining correction (Prov 13:18, 15:5 & 31–33) and of acting impulsively (Prov 14:17 & 29, 16:32, 17:27–28, 18:13, 19:11, 21:5, 25:8–10 & 28, 29:11 & 20, Eccl 7:9, Jas 1:19).

As church leaders we are wise to evaluate and upgrade our own habits and to help others do so as well. We know this on the principle level. Scripture overarchingly teaches us to give our best to God (Gen 4:4–5, Deut 15:19–21, Mal 1:7–9, Matt 22:37, Eph 6:5–8, Col 3:22–24). As leaders we don't want to keep any habit that diminishes our influence or credibility. We want to model Christlikeness (1 Cor 11:1, Eph 4:11, Phil 3:17).

TAKING OUR HABITS TO THE NEXT LEVEL

How do we change a less-than-desirable habit? In several important senses, the best answer is "it depends." Is the habit a sin, like lying or gossip (Exod 20:15–16, John 8:44, Eph 4:25)? The Christian response to sin is repentance. We acknowledge the sin, confess it to God, and change our behavior. Our goal isn't compromise, reduction, or moderation. To be blunt, we go to war against it. We seek God's help and assistance from others, but we know that we must change (Ps 51, Matt 3:8, Luke 13:1–5, Acts 17:30–31). What steps would this involve?

- If the Bible identifies the behavior as sinful, note that fact and be convicted.
- Commit to stopping the behavior. Admittedly, habits are entrenched. There will be a battle. It makes no sense to fight this battle alone.
- We share our commitment with trusted friends and ask them to help us. Prayer, encouragement, and accountability are essential. Friends often share stories and

actions that helped them overcome specific sins.
- Celebrate each victory. Give God thanks.
- It's especially difficult to extinguish a behavior without replacing it. Our goal is never to stop sinning in order to reach some neutral state. Ephesians 4:28 offers direct help. Those who stole are to stop, go to work, and start sharing with those who are in need. The "shift" is not from taking to not taking. There's change of behavior and mindset. We both reject taking and embrace giving.
- We use what we learn to help others. This brings an extra measure of gratitude and victory. What if the habit is less than desirable, but does not sink to the level of sin? In the spirit of giving our best to God and modeling Christlikeness, we seek to upgrade.
- Research may be needed. What is there about my current habit that I find inferior? Wherein is it lacking? Have I seen others exhibit superior behavior? Have I asked them about their choices and commitments? The Bible offers precedent. Jesus's disciples did not ask, "Lord, teach us to pray" because prayer was foreign to them or their culture. At least in part, they asked because they saw something superior, something admirably different about Jesus's prayer life (Luke 11:1).
- When God has not specified a given behavior, we have great freedom to choose. Brainstorming might be wise. If we want to

become more grateful, for example, what options exist? Among the possibilities are text, email, social media post, written note, call, and face-to-face expression. On another level, options include contemplation of the benefits of gratitude, Bible study focused on examples of gratitude, journaling about ways we see others expressing gratitude, remembering how good we feel when people express gratitude to us, asking trusted people to remind us to express our gratitude, seeking advice from a friend who's known for thankfulness, and asking God to make us more grateful. While it won't work for everyone, there's even studying biblical examples of ingratitude and contemplating the costs of being unthankful.
- In terms of specific application, upgrading habits may include a degree of trial and error. Suppose we want to upgrade the depth and quality of our prayer life. We note Mark 1:35 and decide to set the clock half an hour earlier and begin the day with an early morning devotion. That may work well for many, but for some, attention and energy levels will be higher in the evening. It's not going to be one-size-fits-all.

CAVEATS

Upgrading inferior habits is wise so long as we avoid imbalance and perfectionism. We could become so focused on increasing our thankfulness that we judge ourselves harshly for "not being better at it" and fall into discouragement. We could judge ourselves unfairly for not making progress at some arbitrary and unrealistic rate that we unwisely chose. Patience is a major virtue. God's patience with humanity is remarkable. Think of the zigzags within Abraham's journey of faith. Think of the Lord's patience with Peter.

Another form of imbalance might be labeled "compartmental compensation." In its rawest form, it thinks (but never actually says), "Since I'm not good at and don't enjoy encouraging others, I'll make up for that by increasing my weekly financial contribution." Discipleship doesn't work that way. The biblical commission is to seek "the measure of the stature of the fullness of Christ" (Eph 4:13). "Compartmental compensation" doesn't even work on a common-sense level. It's like saying, "Since I'm not good at and don't enjoy fixing electrical problems, I'll paint the trim on the house more often." Jesus called out the Pharisees for their hypocritical practice of this imbalance (Matt 23:23–24).

Some non-sinful habits are clearly worth upgrading. Others may not offer sufficient return on investment. We're not wise enough to offer clear and quantifiable rules, but we strongly believe that the law of diminishing returns applies in some cases. The warning here is to avoid majoring in minors. We dare not bind burdens—on ourselves or on others—that the Lord has not bound (Matt 23:14–15). We dare not choose habits for the sake of being accounted special by others (Matt 23:5–12).

No habit, no matter how godly or beneficial, is beyond Satan's ability to corrupt. The habit of being helpful to others can devolve into excusing and enabling. Exemplary dietary habits can morph into ridiculing or condemning those who don't share those habits. One could give financially to the point of harming his family. Even the habit of prayer could become extreme if we only pray and fail to serve (Jas 2:14–26).

ESSENTIAL SPIRITUAL HABITS

Practice contemplation of God's goodness and purpose (Ps 103, 136, 139). We've heard all our lives, "Get God right, and you'll get life right." Nothing is more foundational than a biblical concept of God. We're blessed to awaken each morning with God on our minds and to end each day thanking Him.

Prayer. The Bible does not specify a given number of daily prayer times. We love the concept of being ceaselessly prayerful (Eph 6:18, 1Thess 5:18, 1 Tim 2:1–6).

Daily Bible study. Again, the Bible does not specify the daily time to be devoted to God's word, but Psalm 119 offers amazing insight:

- "I have stored up Your word in my heart, that I might not sin against You" (119:11).
- "I will meditate on Your precepts and fix my eyes on Your ways. I will delight in Your statutes; I will not forget Your word" (119:15–16).
- "Oh how I love Your law! It is my meditation all the day" (119:97).
- "Your testimonies are my heritage forever, for they are the joy of my heart. I incline my

heart to perform Your statutes forever to the end" (119:111–112).
- "My eyes are awake before the searches of the night that I may meditate on your promise" (119:148).

Dreaming of heaven. Is any language in Scripture more moving than John 14:1–6 and Revelation 21:1–27? Nothing sustains hope like confident expectation of eternity with God in heaven.

Feeling and expressing love (John 3:16–17, 13:34–35, 15:12–13; 1 John 3:16–18, 4:19–21). Love is expressed in countless ways including assistance, attention, concern, empathy, forgiveness, patience, support, and teaching (1 Cor 13).

Feeling and expressing gratitude. "In everything by prayer and supplication with thanksgiving let your requests be made known to God" (Phil 4:6). "Give thanks in all circumstances, for this is the will of God in Christ Jesus for you" (1 Thess 5:18). Where there is gratitude, there will be joy.

Encouraging others (Rom 1:8–13, Phil 2:3–4, Heb 10:24). What can be more encouraging than sharing in the mission of Christ (Acts 2:42–47, 2 Cor 5:12–21)?

Doing the good that we can (Matt 5:13–16, 20:25–28; Gal 6:9–10, Phil 2:12–13, Titus 2:14, 1 Pet 2:11–12). Implementation idea: Commit to doing at least one good deed to God's glory each day. Making the commitment will cause the brain to look for opportunities to fulfill it. The heightened awareness will bless in impressive ways.

Seeing the good in God's world (Gen 1:31, Ps 19, Prov 30:24–31, Luke 1:25–38, 2 Cor 8:1–5, Rev 2:8–11). Implementation idea: Commit to keeping a joy book. Only joyful entries are allowed. Each day, at least one entry will be added. As above, making the commitment will raise awareness of happy thoughts, sights, and events. As a bonus, take the time to thank God as each joy is noticed.

Thinking before we speak (Prov 10:19, 18:13; Jas 1:19). Is a word needed? If so, what word? How might what I'm thinking of saying be received? Is there a kinder wording, a phrasing that's gentler but just as effective (Prov 15:1–2)? Is this how I'd want someone to talk to me (Matt 7:12)? Is this the best time and place for these words (Prov 25:11–12, Eccl 3:7)?

Saying less than we think (Prov 17:27–28, 29:11). Sometimes silence is the safest course, the wisest action, and the kindest gift (Job 2:11–13).

Acting better than we feel (Matt 5:43–48). To state this virtue more fully, we mean doing what's right no matter how we feel in the moment (Matt 26:36–42, Heb 12:1–2).

Doing more than we have to, going the second mile (Matt 5:38–42, Phil 2:5–11). From common courtesy to sacrificial giving, God will never allow a giver to go unblessed (Acts 20:35). To sow sparingly guarantees a thin harvest (2 Cor 9:6).

FOUNDATIONALLY, WHAT DOES IT TAKE TO CHANGE A HABIT?

We won't seek to improve a habit unless we perceive sufficient motivation. For Christians, that motivation comes in many forms.

- If we come to see any action as sinful, there's plenty of motivation for change (Rom 6:3, 2 Cor 5:10–11).
- If we come to see a change as God-honoring, there's equal positive motivation for improvement (1 Cor 15:58, Titus 2:14, 2 Pet 1:8–11).
- If we believe a change will bless those we love, we're moved to act (1 Tim 4:12–16).
- We can be moved to attempt improvement in support of a friend who wants to change and requests our partnership.

Most of us won't seek to improve a habit unless we believe the change is possible. There may be rare exceptions who act out of duty or loyalty even in the face of hopelessness, but they are few (John 11:16). Most won't attempt what they believe to be impossible.

As a rule, we won't work to change a habit unless we believe the change will be worth our effort. Whether we think in terms of risk vs. reward or return on investment, we ask ourselves, "Will there be sufficient benefit?" Faith gives Christians notable advantage in this area (Rom 1:17, 2 Cor 4:7, Heb 11:1 & 6). We believe that any good we do flows from and is enabled by God (Phil 2:12–13). We're never alone in the process of growth.

Additionally, we don't know what doors God will open; we don't even know all the doors that He has already opened. A beloved friend who is now with the Lord, Basil Overton, greatly enjoyed saying, "I love what I'm doing because I don't know what I'm doing." That was never a claim of incompetence. Rather, it employed ellipsis to invite thought. The fuller version would be, "I love what I'm doing for God because I don't know all the wondrous ways God might choose to use what I'm doing." That concept rings true for Christians as we choose to grow with God's help to God's glory.

As implied twice above, most of us won't attempt challenging change if we believe we'll have to do it alone. Again, there's major advantage for Christians. God stands with us and helps us more than we can even dream. Also, God adds the saved to His church, so we have family who can help us as well (Acts 2:47, 2 Tim 1:3–7, Heb 10:24). We live within God's kingdom, where people who share our precious faith love to see us grow and excel (Rom 12:10–16, 2 Pet 1:1).

PRACTICALLY, WHAT DOES IT TAKE TO CHANGE A HABIT?

Christians will always begin with prayer. We ask God to help us understand His will and our needs (Ps 139:23–24). We ask God for wisdom (Jas 1:5). We ask God for strength and stamina.

While we ask God to help us understand our needs, we also employ self-evaluation (2 Cor 13:5). Knowing our tendency to self-bias, we ask trusted others for insight (Prov 21:2). Since no humans are infallible, we keep God's word as our touchstone as we evaluate information and suggestions.

We make a commitment to change and share that commitment with people who can help us. We welcome their input, encouragement, and correction. Have they made similar improvements? If so, what tools and techniques worked for them? What obstacles did they encounter? How were those obstacles overcome? Were there temptations to give up? Even after the new habit was in place, were there temptations to revert to the old ways? How were those temptations overcome?

The literature varies notably, but some say a new habit can be ingrained in 14 days. Others say 28. It's likely that there is no consistent timing. It's reasonable to assume that the timing will vary depending on how major the change is, the level and consistency of support for the change, the personality of the person making the change, and the perception of benefit from the change. The real deal isn't the number of days that it takes. Far more important is the fact that positive change is possible. Good habits make excellent servants, but bad ones make terrible masters. Any habit that detracts from our service to God can—with His help—be changed to His glory.

ENDNOTES

[1] This chapter resonates with sister chapters "Wellness" and "Helping People Who Are Stuck."

CHAPTER 17
WHEN WE MUST SHARE BAD NEWS

As Christian leaders, we want people to be well, whole, and blessed. We love to tell the good, and we hate to be bearers of bad news. We find joy in seeing others happy. But in this sin-damaged world, much lies beyond our control. In this fallen world, all the news isn't good.

Why would we state such an obvious truth? We need the reminder that even strong Christians sometimes forget it during challenging times. Some even refer to Scripture as they forget:

- "Ask, and it will be given to you; seek, and you will find; knock, and the door will be opened to you" (Matt 7:7).
- "Again I say to you, if two of you agree on earth about anything you ask, it will be done for them by My Father in heaven" (Matt 18:19).
- "Love never fails" (1 Cor 13:8, NJKV).

- "I can do all things through Him who strengthens me" (Phil 4:13).

Especially during crises, people forget to read such verses in context and in balance with the whole of biblical teaching (Matt 26:36–39, 2 Cor 12:7–10). Jesus's prayer was not answered by avoiding the cross. Paul's "thorn" was not removed. Regarding Philippians 4:13, the context strongly supports the understanding of "I can endure all things through Christ who strengthens me." As much as faith, attitude, and perspective matter, Paul is not endorsing the absolute power of positive thinking. The Bible does not teach that reality bends to our preferences. Reality does not change because we want it to.

Some problems are intractable; they do not have solutions on this planet. Other problems have only partial solutions. Sometimes people come to us for help with meeting unrealistic expectations. What they want is simply not achievable. Easy examples include wanting a job—world-class musician or baseball star—for which they lack the talent or physicality. A much tougher example is wanting a loved one to become a Christian, overcome addiction, and lead a blessed life. It's tougher because our loved one could make those choices; they lie within the realm of possibility. It's also tougher because those choices are outside our control. Unless the person wants God's help and chooses God's way, the blessings will not come.

PERSPECTIVES ON NEGATIVE NEWS

Those we try to help do not all share the same perspective on negative news regarding the difficult issues that they face. Some come to us with a firm grasp of reality. They know they can't make others change. They know that some diseases have no cure. For them, "what is, is" and must be dealt with. They make our lives easier as counselors.

Others are unsure of the nature of their challenges. They may not yet have sorted things we can change as opposed to things that are beyond our control. They may not yet have differentiated problems they—at least to some degree—have caused versus bad things that have happened to them. They need assistance with exploration and understanding.

Think of Job and his friends. The friends were certain that Job brought about his own misery (Job 4:7–9). Job was just as certain that he loved God and lived righteously (Job 7:20–21). Neither Job nor his friends knew of the greater conversation between God and Satan (Job 1:6–2:7). Because of their foundational error, Job's friends became miserable helpers (accusers, afflicters) who offered him no comfort at all. We see a similar errant assumption by Jesus's apostles in John 9:1–3.

The most challenging group, for whatever reason, denies reality. Those individuals believe every problem has a solution. The quest is to find that answer, no matter the cost. For a church leader to question these people's thinking may be viewed as lack of faith, disbelief in the power of prayer, and/or unwillingness to try.

To offer an example, a husband comes wanting assistance in saving his marriage—a most noble goal. He says to you, "I love my God, I love my wife, and with your help I will save my marriage." And you reply, "I will do my best to help." There's obvious dismay, "What do you mean, 'Do your best'? Don't you believe marriage is forever and God hates divorce (Gen 2:24, Mal 2:16, Matt 19:4–6)? Why do I hear doubt in your words?"

We support marriage and know that God holds all power. We also know that while it takes two to marry, one can decide to leave. As lamentable as it is, the husband could do everything within his power to save his marriage, and his wife could choose to end it anyway. How do we help such a person come to understand such painful truth? Similarly, even a wonderful set of Christian parents cannot believe enough, try enough, do enough, or love enough to guarantee the righteous behavior of their children (Ezek 18).

We hope we have made the case that as leaders who try to help hurting people, one of our first needs is assessment. We need to learn; we dare not assume that we understand the issue or the need (Prov 18:13). Do these hurting people have a biblically-informed mindset? Do they know what they can control (their own attitude and behavior) versus what they can't (the behavior and attitude of others, much of the physical reality around us)? Are they able to keep their expectations realistic? Do they know that God still offers amazing help to the disappointed and broken-hearted (Ps 145:8–21)?

A SECOND SET OF PERSPECTIVES

Those who come to us for help with intractable issues may not know whether or how much to trust us. This leads to a second set of perspectives on bad news. Some honest hurting souls don't come to us for answers to their problems. They know full answers don't exist in this life. They share their pain with us for two reasons. First, they need for someone to know, care, and pray. Second, they need to learn whether they can trust us.

- Are we willing to accept our limitations, to admit that we don't "fix people"?
- Are we willing to hold onto God and faith when faced with complex needs that we can't fully understand?
- Are we mature enough to stay silent when we should, to avoid offering false answers?
- Will we be fair, honest, and loving, no matter what?

In this regard, how we deal with the disclosure and telling of negative information is a test of our character, faithfulness, and maturity. We dare not fail the test.

Some who seek our help are not so noble and honest. Rather than testing our faith and honesty, they come seeking absolution. Like the shallow people described by Paul, "having itching ears they will accumulate for themselves teachers to suit their own passions" (2 Tim 4:3). Their intent is not understanding, repentance, and restoration. Their intent is to dodge truth and responsibility. We dare not assist them in this futile venture.

Bluntly, some love it when a church leader tells them what they want to hear—even when they know the message is false. There have always been some who prefer myth to truth (2 Tim 4:4). We dare not be among them (John 8:31–32, 2 Thess 3:11–12).

As you have likely noticed, this chapter deals with at least two categories of "bad news" commonly encountered in counseling. The major category is what we describe as intractable problems—problems that have no full solution here and now. These include cases where relationships cannot be maintained or restored because the other party is deceased or unwilling, physical issues (loss of health) that cannot be changed, loved ones who will not choose godliness, and lost dreams. Think of Joseph's separation from his people, Job's tragic losses, David's loss of relationship with King Saul, Daniel's captivity, and Paul's strong desire that all Israel be saved.

A second category is damage which we caused or helped cause. We stand responsible for our words, actions, and attitudes. Think of Peter denying Jesus, Saul of Tarsus consenting to the death of Stephen, or the church in Corinth descending into division. While we can repent, be utterly forgiven, and do better, we cannot always undo the consequences of past sins and errors.

BAD OPTIONS FOR DEALING WITH NEGATIVE NEWS

What are the options in counseling when we cannot give people the good news that they crave? The horrible options include lying, which of course would be relabeled as "sparing their feelings" or "protecting them."

We can't lie and be right with God (Eph 4:25, Rev 21:8). Ultimately, we can't help people by lying.

Almost as bad is saying little and hoping the people we're helping won't notice. That's a fundamental insult. There is biblical support for using discretion and not always saying everything that we think. Only a fool verbally vents every feeling (Prov 29:11). But there is no biblical support for withholding needed truth (Acts 20:26–27, Gal 4:16).

A softer version is hinting at the truth and hoping that they'll figure it out. We love the respect and growth orientation of guided discovery. We recommend and support that process. However, we hate and fear cowardice. As godly leaders, we cannot leave people floundering when they need a clear word of truth.

Another bad option is offering hollow platitudes. "Yes, your loss is great, but think of all the blessings that you still have." "One day, you'll look back on this and smile." "We all must accept the bad with the good." "It'll all work out in the end."

A final poor choice is offering foolish comparisons. "Yes, your situation is bad, but it's not nearly as tragic and pervasive as Job's." "Tough as it is, your life comes nowhere close to the cruelty and injustice that Jesus endured." "We both know people who've suffered more." Even if true, such words in a time of great pain offer neither insight nor comfort. They sound callous and dismissive. Such words are often perceived as insult or attack.

AN EVEN WORSE ALTERNATIVE

What could be worse than the terrible options listed above? Two foundational issues come to mind. First, we hear rare reports of church leaders who seem to enjoy delivering negative news to hurting people. This is sometimes mislabeled as courage, tough love, or letting the chips fall where they may. It's accompanied by language like "They're reaping what they have sown." "They brought this on themselves." "The pain will remind them not to do this again."

Such thinking does not accord with love, grace, mercy, or compassion (Mic 6:8, John 13:24-35, Eph 4:29-32). It seems to flow from a false dichotomy of "I can either tell the truth or be kind and caring." Scripture strongly supports caring, kindness, and truth.

A second fierce danger is embodied in the statement that a church leader once made to a couple seeking his help: "I can help you. I can guarantee that your marriage will survive and grow stronger if you will agree to do everything that I tell you." The leader may have meant this as a statement of confidence, but we hear it as tragic arrogance and ignorance. We love counselors who promise prayer and effort. We fear counselors who guarantee results. Even Jesus did not secure the best outcome with everyone He encountered (Mark 10:17-22).

There are far better options when we must share difficult news with those we counsel. We begin by praying for wisdom (James 1:5). Pray for the wisdom to ask the right questions in the best ways at the right time. Pray for the wisdom to maintain humility and to continue learning. Pray for wisdom to stay out of God's way as He works to bless.

Speak the truth in love (John 13:34–35, Eph 4:15, Col 3:6). No lies, no hedging, no making of excuses. Any lie dishonors God, self, and the person with whom we're working.

Speak in the way that we'd want someone to speak to us (Matt 7:12). Try to look to their interest (Phil 2:3–4). Even imperfect efforts to honor this principle carry great weight. We have worked with people who notice both our effort to speak their language and our inadequacy at doing so. On multiple occasions, they have expressed appreciation for the attempt and even helped us find the proper words. It's a wonderful paradox where the "helpee" becomes, at least for the moment, the helper, and everybody gets blessed. It's amazing when God uses even our inadequacies to make us more effective helpers.

Speak in language that the person we're helping is capable of hearing (Prov 25:11–12). Within God's will, Paul clearly adapted his ministry to various social and cultural settings (1 Cor 9:19–23).

Use stories (a narrative approach) when a story is most appropriate. The prophet Nathan accomplished through a pitch-perfect story what might have been impossible through any other means (2 Sam 12:1–6). Even imperfect stories still hold great power. Using them to help others calls for the highest level of discernment. It demands wisdom and experience.

When the truth needs to be clearly stated, find the courage and state the truth (2 Sam 12:7). Do not leave truth in doubt. Nathan's, "You are the man!" was not a "gotcha" moment when the prophet put the king in his place. Rather, it was a courageous statement paving the way for a clear and complete disclosure of God's word.

Use questions to open minds and promote reflection (1 Kings 19:9 & 13). NOTE: 1 Kings 19 does not stand in opposition to 2 Samuel 12. These examples present different skills that fit different contexts.

Do nothing harshly. It is not our role to punish (John 8:10–11, Rom 12:15–21). Good people already feel terrible if they have helped cause pain. Godly grief has already worked repentance (2 Cor 7:10). Nothing is gained by doubling down on sorrow when repentance has already occurred.

Don't argue. If the person we're helping can't hear us yet, we wait. Show all patience (Titus 3:1–7). Sometimes we start to say what we believe to be wise in the moment but come to realize that the time is not yet right. We humbly self-correct and wait. Though the context has nothing to do with counseling, Paul sets a strong example of this attitude in Acts 23:1–5.

Tell the truth, but offer only realistic hope. Offer no false dreams. As with Paul in 2 Corinthians 12, the "solution" may not be deliverance or removal of the problem. The solution may be choosing, with God's help, to accept reality. On a higher level, the solution may be a change of attitude and perspective (reframing) to align our thinking with God's (Isa 55:8–9).

Tell the truth, and offer ongoing support. Don't desert those whose needs and issues have no easy answer (2 Cor 1:3–4, Gal 6:9–10, 1 Thess 5:14). We're blessed to "bear one another's burdens, and so fulfill the law of Christ," and to honor the principle that "each one will have to bear his own load" (Gal 6:2 & 5). Again, there's tremendous blessing in wisdom and balance.

When the heart's door opens and the time is right, affirm God's ultimate deliverance. Everything will be right in God's tomorrow (2 Cor 4:16–5:7). There's coming a day when God Himself will wipe away every tear (Rev 21:4). Warning: to present this truth prematurely will rob it of its power.

It has been proposed that we can help and comfort others only as far as our ability to endure pain will allow (2 Cor 12:28–29). While that's not the whole story, it contains an important element of truth. Helping others means entering their world and sharing their pain. It also includes realizing that we can't always end that pain. Sometimes, we face great challenge even in our efforts to ease it. To be blunt, sometimes people feel worse before they feel better. Sometimes improvement is both microscopic and stunningly slow.

Still, there's nobility in trying to help others. There's nobility in loving. And there's wisdom in trying and loving God's way. God bless your every faithful effort!

CHAPTER 18

DEALING WITH TOXIC PEOPLE

As much as we appreciate the fundamental worth of people (Gen 1:26–27, Psalm 8, John 3:16), we know better than to assert the fundamental goodness of all people (Rom 1:18–32, 3:9–18). Toxic people exist. By "toxic" we mean tempting, discouraging, and spiritually/morally dangerous. We speak of those who make it easier to do wrong and harder to live right. Toxic relationships are those that consistently endanger our well-being and spiritual health.

It's impressive to note the frequency with which the Bible directly warns against bad influences and dangerous relationships (Prov 1:10–19, 12:5–6 & 26, 13:20, 16:27–30, 22:24–25, 23:20–21, 24:1, 27:21–22; Matt 16:5–12; 1 Cor 15:33; 2 Tim 3:1–5). We add to the direct warnings the many biblical examples of destructive relationships. Job's friends became punishing accusers as they challenged his faithfulness (Job 4:7–10, 8:1–7, 11:1–6). Would Amnon have assaulted his sister if the crafty Jonadab had not plotted the evil act (2 Sam 13:1–20)? Would Ahab have been as much of an evil and murderous tyrant without Jezebel's influence (1 Kgs 21)? Would the weak kings of Jeremiah's day have been so faithless without their cadre of false prophets (Jer 23:9-40, 29:1-23)? Would the crowd that demanded the death of Jesus have done so without "encouragement" (Mark 15:11-15)? Virtually everyone has witnessed situations worsen through the influence of "bad actors."

ANYBODY CAN BE TOXIC

Regrettably, anyone can be toxic toward others. Eve became toxic when she invited Adam to share in her sin (Gen 3:6). Adam became toxic when he blamed Eve for his sin (Gen 3:12). Cain's toxicity reached its apex in the murder of his brother (Gen 4:8). Even righteous Abraham became toxic as he endangered both Pharaoh and then Abimelech through his lies (Gen 12:10-29, 20:1-18). We'd say the same of Peter as he attempted, perhaps out of the best of motives, to counter Jesus's words and thwart His mission (Matt 16:21-23). Galatians 2:11-21 offers a similar example when Peter's poor actions led even Barnabas to err.

The purpose of this chapter is not to encourage labeling or judgmentalism. In part, it seeks to encourage us to watch our own motives and actions (Matt 7:1-4, John 7:24). Leaders, including church leaders, commonly have disproportionate influence. Bluntly, we sometimes carry considerable weight. Used for good, that's excellent (1 Cor 11:1, Phil 3:17 & 4:9, 1 Tim 4:12-16). Misused, the damage is stunningly multiplied (Matt 7:15, 2 Tim 4:3-4, Jude 3-10, Rev 2:20-23).

The first logical step in helping people deal with toxic relationships is to personally model holiness, purity, and love. The second is to know, love, and teach "the whole counsel of God" (Acts 20:27). The third is to teach God's truth practically. There's value in knowing how to identify toxic actions and toxic people. There's value in learning to protect both ourselves and others from both.

LEVELS OF TOXIC RELATIONSHIPS

The closer a relationship, the greater its power. Generally, we grant strangers little influence, friends far more, and family most of all.

What if we find ourselves harmed by people who don't reach the level of "friend"? As much as is feasible, we limit contact and minimize their influence. As much as is possible, we choose to let their comments and actions flow like water off a duck's back. We do not give them power in our lives. Among the healthy self-talk regarding toxic strangers and acquaintances is, "I'm not giving you any space in my head," and "I won't give you the power to ruin my day."

What if we find ourselves being harmed by toxic friends? On the upside, a modern proverb reminds us: "Friends are family that we choose for ourselves." If certain friends are toxic, we need to make better choices. If wise, we review our friend selection process. What do we need to improve? What do we know now that we didn't know then? How can we be smarter next time?

We're not advocating disposable friendships where

any sign of trouble ends the relationship. We are affirming that if a friendship is justly found to be toxic and the toxic party is unwilling to change, wisdom demands that the relationship end. We help ourselves and others find the courage to do what wisdom demands.

Our families of origin influence us heavily before we possess any hint of awareness that they are shaping us. God created family to bless and nurture (Gen 2:18 & 21–24 and 4:1; Ps 127:3–5; Prov 12:4, 18:22, 19:14, 31:10–31). All who were brought up "in the discipline and instruction of the Lord" are blessed beyond measure (Gen 18:18–19, Deut 6:4–9, Eph 6:4). Our hearts go out to people who were reared in toxic families. We utterly oppose abuse, cruelty, and neglect (Prov 29:15). We lack the ability to express the level of our respect for those who were reared in toxic homes and—with God's help—overcame that rearing. We know this is possible both from Ezekiel 18 and from observation. We also know something of how rare and difficult it is.

Another key to helping people deal with toxic relationships is understanding that whatever we grew up seeing and believing is normal to us. For some, even as adults, it's all they know. Those who lived and learned unbiblical patterns will need major education. They will need to know that better options exist and that change is possible. Please do not assume that everyone knows this.

We love to encourage and compliment people we call "stoppers." Stoppers are those who identify and stop toxic patterns. They move from harmful habits and through neutral habits all the way to loving and soul-affirming behaviors. They raise the bar not only for themselves but for future generations. We find these good people to be amazing.

Even people who have largely overcome bad parenting are likely to maintain vestiges of the bad patterns. They are likely to maintain some errant beliefs and some dysfunctional behaviors. As church leaders, we are wise to compliment their growth. We're also wise to offer insight regarding avenues of continued growth. For example, a son may have endured a physically abusive father. As an adult, he has rejected physical violence, but he verbally abuses his own family. Compliment the progress, but don't settle. Educate regarding the MAJOR harm of verbal abuse. Teach communication patterns that are consistent with Ephesians 4:29-32 and Colossians 4:6. The first step in teaching is to model those patterns ourselves.

Just as our families of origin shape us, we shape and are shaped by our current family system. It's fair to ask, "What do I do if my spouse or other family members are toxic?" There are no easy answers. Ideally, we'd love to have people pose this question before the dating/mate selection process begins. Then, we'd say the following:

- Be a Christian, faithful and committed. This will help you attract friends who also love God.
- Date only people who love God and show it.
- Go slow. People of quality will be patient with you.
- Keep your eyes open and your mind in gear. When something isn't right, note it. Explore

it. Is this a minor issue that needs correction? Is your help welcome? If the person lies, denies, or blows up at the prospect of being asked to improve, run.

"Nice list, but way too late for me. I'm married, and aspects of my marriage are toxic. What can I do?"

- Be the best you can be for Jesus. Family is a system. As any part of the system improves, it invites the whole system to improve. Most people live reciprocally. The better we treat them, the better they treat us. Neither forget nor underestimate the power of a godly example (1 Pet 3:1–12).
- Pray for strength, mercy, endurance, and encouragement.
- Resist the temptation to devolve. Don't sink to their level. God's will is to "overcome evil with good" (Rom 12:21).

CAVEATS

To recognize the shortcomings of our parents is not to disown them. We can still appreciate all their good qualities. We keep loving them. We show them the honor that God commands (Eph 6:1–3). Our purpose is not to condemn, but to assess and improve.

In that no one comes from a perfect home, we all have things to unlearn and improve. We waste time and energy if we choose to blame our parents, spouse, children, siblings, or friends for our current struggles. If they bear blame before God, we leave judgment and justice to Him (Rom 12:17–21). We rightly celebrate every blessing gained from our families of origin and our current families. But we don't close our eyes to the opportunity to do better.

TYPES OF TOXIC PEOPLE

There is an extensive and helpful literature of dealing with toxic/difficult people. While those mentioned here are older, they have not lost their edge. From an everyday perspective, Bramson's *Coping with Difficult People* is outstanding.[1] From a biblical viewpoint, there's *Don't Let Jerks Get the Best of You*[2] and *High Maintenance Relationships*.[3] More narrowly focused is *The Verbally Abusive Relationship*.[4] From a broader perspective, it is difficult to improve on *Boundaries*.[5]

Some of the literature creatively labels the types of difficult/toxic people and groups, for example the cold shoulder, the flirt, the negativist, and the sniper. We can appreciate the concept of battling pain through humor. We don't find those labels mean or demeaning, but we offer a more categorical view.

From one perspective, there are two major types of toxic people, the self-aware and the unaware. The unaware can benefit from insight and education. There's little path for improvement for those who are toxic, know it, and have accepted that as part of their nature. They are people we visit in small doses. We schedule appointments adjacent to those visits so that we have legitimate reasons to escape. We don't kid ourselves; we know that no one can endure major contact without major damage.

Alternately, there are many types and subtypes of difficult people. For example, the hypercritical can be hypercritical of everything and/or everyone, hypercritical of select others, or hypercritical predominately of themselves. Every form will be characterized by discouragement, negativity, pessimism, and lack of balance. But some who are hyper-self-critical will just want you to listen, neither agreeing nor objecting. Others will want you to present a more optimistic view so that they feel slightly better in the moment. Some will want you to argue with their pessimism so that they can double down and sharpen their negative skills.

Some who are hypercritical of others have the courage to express their disappointments directly to those with whom they are disappointed. Conversations with them can begin by acknowledging that courage. Others will express their negativity to everyone except the person to whom they should be speaking. They present an even greater challenge.

Some toxic people are fundamentally angry with the universe, including God and themselves. Others seem to think quite highly of themselves; it's the rest of us who need fixing. A combination of anger and arrogance is extremely off-putting. A major challenge in attempting to help such people is managing our own anger. We can offer several possible techniques for dealing with these bullies.

- Prayer. Pray for wisdom, patience, and perseverance.

- Physical monitoring. Is blood pressure okay? Am I remembering to breathe normally? Am I experiencing an adrenaline rush that's inviting a fight-or-flight choice? Do I need a sip of water? Just staying aware helps. A bit of bio-feedback (stay calm, breathe slowly, no panic) can help.
- Sound thinking-1. When faced with a bully, it's powerful to remember: "You're not the boss of me. I'll let you express your pain or explain your position, but God has not put me under your control." A superior version of this message-to-self for Christians is "I work for God. He's the better boss. If God is pleased with me, I'm good." We believe Paul does this in 1 Corinthians 4:1–5.
- Sound thinking-2. Likely, you have been in similar pressurized situations before. You did not die. No one died. You survived. You even learned some things that can help you deal with the current crisis.
- Sound thinking-3. Whether the demand of the moment is "Fix this," "Make this better," or "Promise me that you'll fix it," balk. Unless the responsibility is yours, refuse to accept it. Sometimes, it may be necessary to say, "I'm sorry. This is beyond my ability" or "I can't rightly agree to be responsible for this." In other situations, we "slow play." We simply don't promise what we shouldn't promise. If pushed, a tried and true response is "I'll need to give this thought and prayer."

- Sound thinking-4. Ask pertinent questions. Often difficult people practice tunnel vision and create false dichotomies. Tunnel vision is missing the broader picture by taking an extremely narrow view. Think of viewing a panoramic scene with one eye though a narrow tube. There's no way to grasp the scene fully. False dichotomy is imagining or pretending that only two choices exist—black/white, yes/no—when there are more options. For example: "I'm allergic to her perfume. Either you tell her to quit wearing it or I'm not coming back to worship." An obvious alternative would be to change where you sit. If the toxic person will consider alternatives, progress is possible. If not, recognize that their goal is neither improvement nor solution. If their goal is to win or to "get my way," then biblical precepts aren't being honored (1 Cor 12, Phil 2:1–4).

WHY NOT JUST LET THE TOXIC PERSON WIN?

There are biblical examples of choosing to lose. Paul asked Corinthian Christians who were battling brothers in court, "Why nor rather suffer wrong? Why not rather be defrauded?" (1 Cor 6:7) Similarly, Matthew records Jesus acting so as to avoid offending those demanding payment of the temple tax (Matt 17:24–27). Paul personally circumcised Timothy to avoid having issues of his Greek-Jewish parentage hinder the gospel (Acts 16:1–3).

As a matter of principle, Christians don't live offensively (Prov 18:19, Rom 12:18, Gal 5:22-23, Titus 2:24-26).

There's nobility and humility in sacrifice and suffering for the sake of the kingdom (Heb 10:32-34; 1 Pet 3:14, 4:16). It's always wise to trust God to care for us. We never value image or possessions over kindness and love.

On the other hand, there are biblical examples of costly refusal to compromise truth or mistreat others. The Hebrew midwives rightly disobeyed Pharaoh's order to kill male Jewish babies (Exod 1:15-22). Shadrach, Meshach, and Abednego stood faithful even as the king took deadly offense at their choice not to bow to his image (Dan 3:8-23).

As He taught the parables recorded in Matthew 13, Jesus was unfazed when His hearers "took offense at Him." They took offense, though He offered none. The issue was theirs, not His. Jesus also offered no apology when His disciples asked, "Do you know that the Pharisees were offended when they heard this saying?" (Matt 15:12). Jesus offered no apology for speaking God's truth.

When Peter and others withheld fellowship with Gentile Christians due to the presence of Jewish visitors, Paul "opposed him to his face" ... "because their conduct was not in step with the truth of the gospel" (Gal 2:11 & 14). Paul did not feel compelled to circumcise Titus—no doubt disappointing some Jews and offending others—explaining, "to them we did not yield in submission even for a moment so that the truth of the gospel might be preserved for you ..." (Gal 2:1-10). Paul would make no law where God had made none.

There are situations where letting an ignorant or

toxic person prevail is kind, wise, sacrificial, and peace-seeking (Matt 5:9, Rom 12:18, Jas 3:13–18, 1 Pet 3:8–18). In other circumstances, to compromise or submit would dishonor God. We can never rightly act counter to God's truth.

Even from a common-sense point of view, at times we don't oppose (at least not in an ongoing public manner) a toxic person (Prov 26:4–5, Titus 3:9–11). Thankfully, the toxic are sometimes sufficiently shrill, radical, inconsistent, or obviously wrong that they discredit themselves. On those occasions, our silence speaks louder than our words (Rom 12:16–21, Jude 9). Other situations, however, demand both godly action and a word from the Lord (1 Pet 3:15–16, Jude 3). We honor our commitment to act wisely and faithfully in God's service (Mic 6:8, 1 Cor 15:58).

Bottom line: The first rule of dealing with toxic individuals is "Don't be one." The second, "Thank the Lord that everyone isn't." And the third, "Even the most toxic people can't move us away from God unless we choose to let them" (Rom 8:31–39).

ENDNOTES

[1.] Robert M. Bramson, *Coping with Difficult People* (Garden City, NY: Anchor Press/Doubleday, 1981).

[2.] Paul Meier, *Don't Let Jerks Get the Best of You: Advice for Dealing with Difficult People* (Nashville: Thomas Nelson, 1991).

[3.] Les Parrott, *High Maintenance Relationships: How to Handle Impossible People* (Wheaton, IL: Tyndale House, 1996).

4. Patricia Evans, *The Verbally Abusive Relationship: How to Recognize It and How to Respond*, 2nd ed., (Holbrook, MA: Adams Media Corp, 1996).

5. Henry Cloud and John Townsend, *Boundaries: When to Say Yes, When to Say No to Take Control of Your Life* (Grand Rapids: Zondervan, 1992).

CHAPTER 19
SELF-ESTEEM AND SELFISHNESS
HELPING PEOPLE THINK BIBLICALLY

No wonder many are confused. Even within Bible-believing communities, there's remarkable contradiction in teachings about selfishness and self-esteem. Some see the two as a single errant entity. "It's wrong for a Christian to love himself or herself. It's sinful." On the opposite extreme, some present self-esteem as the key to a happy and fulfilling life. "It's God's will for you to love yourself. Without self-love, it's impossible to love others" (Matt 22:30). At this point, some will cry foul. "You just switched language on us. You wrote about self-esteem and self-love as if those are synonyms. Don't you know that self-love is condemned in 2 Timothy 3:2?" And that verse certainly condemns loving self rather than God.

CONSISTENT OPPOSITION TO SELFISHNESS

From cover to cover, the Bible opposes selfishness. It does so in three major ways. The first is by the unselfish example of God the Father and His faithful followers. From the creation, we see God looking out for Adam's best interest (Gen 2:18). Even after Adam and Eve sinned, God came looking for them (Gen 3). Even as He exiled them from Eden, God clothed and blessed them (Gen 3:21, 4:1). God's record of unselfishness remains unblemished.

We think next of God the Son—"even as the Son of Man came not to be served, but to serve, and to give His life as a ransom for many" (Matt 20:28). Remember the powerful description of Jesus from Philippians 2:5–11: "He made Himself nothing, taking on the form of a servant" and dying for us. Remember how Jesus praised the faith and selflessness of the widow who gave the two small coins and the lady who anointed Him with the expensive flask of oil (Mark 12:41–44, 14:3–9). The parable of the Good Samaritan both describes and invites selfless behavior (Luke 10).

From the Old Testament, we cherish the selfless example set by Ruth (Ruth 1:16–17). We're moved to admiration by Jonathan's selfless embrace of David (1 Sam 18:1–4). In the New Testament, we're impressed to find the first Christians described as sacrificially selfless (Acts 2:44–46, 2 Cor 8:1–7). We love the way big-hearted Barnabas is contrasted with the self-serving Ananias and Sapphira (Acts 4:32–5:11). We take heart from Paul's beautiful description of Timothy: "For I have no one like him, who will be genuinely concerned for your welfare. For they all seek their own interests, not those of Jesus Christ" (Phil 2:20–21).

The second opposition to selfishness is outright condemnation. Jesus taught, "Whoever loves his life loses it, and whoever hates his life in this world will keep it for eternal life." We know to read this truth in light of Luke 9:23–26 and 2 Corinthians 4:16–5:11. This world is not our forever home. This world won't last. Direct opposition to selfishness is evident in the "works of the flesh" from Galatians 5:19–21. At a minimum, strife, jealousy, rivalries, envy, dissensions, and divisions often flow from selfishness.

In addition to those that directly condemn selfishness, several passages strongly warn against it. "But understand this, that in the last days there will come times of difficulty, for people will be lovers of self" (1 Tim 3:1–2). "Do nothing from rivalry or conceit" (Phil 2:3). "But if you have bitter jealously and selfish ambition in your heart, do not boast and be false to the truth ... For where jealousy and selfish ambition exist, there will be disorder and every evil practice" (Jas 3:14 & 16). "For by the grace given to me I say to everyone among you not to think of himself more highly than he ought to think" (Rom 12:3). And there are the stories that reveal the stench of selfishness, from David's disaster with Bathsheba to Ahab committing murder to take Naboth's vineyard (2 Sam 11–12, 1 Kgs 21). Nothing good ever comes of selfishness.

CAVEAT: UNHEALTHY SELFLESSNESS

Satan offers a false version of every virtue. As wholesome and admirable as we find sacrifice and selflessness, even those concepts exist in ungodly forms. Matthew 7:21–23 documents this sad truth. Some who view themselves as having done "many mighty works" in God's name, are not known to God. They are deceived and don't realize that they are practicing lawlessness. Matthew 6:1, 5, and 16 offer examples. Some in Jesus's day practiced benevolence, prayed, and fasted "that they might be seen by others" (Matt 6:5). While their religious practices might have appeared selfless, Jesus knew them to be the opposite. Acts 5 and 2 Timothy 3:5 provide similar warnings.

We draw two major implications. First, we need to check our own motives and seek God's help in doing so (Job 31:5–7, Ps 139:23–24, Matt 7:1–5, 2 Cor 13:5). Then, we need to ensure our compliance with the teachings of God's word (Prov 3:5–8). It's noble to sacrifice to the glory of God, but it's folly to sacrifice for the sake of creating or maintaining an image. What might this look like today? To offer an example that might sound pious but isn't: "I have no life. I've sacrificed everything for my children." An even sadder example: "We could have had a good life, but we gave ourselves to ministry instead." False martyrdom creates stunning prisons.

DANGEROUS VERSIONS OF SELF-ESTEEM

There's little challenge in documenting dangerous versions of self-esteem. As noted above, Scripture commands us not to think of ourselves more highly than we ought to think (Rom 12:3). Biblically, those who esteem themselves too highly don't fare well. Pharaoh invited God's ire by failing to recognize Him as Lord (Exod 5:1–2). The kings of Tyre and Sidon improperly elevated themselves, to the point of claiming, "I am perfect in beauty," and "I am a god, I sit in the seat of the gods," (Ezek 27:3, 28:2). Each city fell to judgment and horrific destruction. For all his good qualities, King Nebuchadnezzar let pride consume him. Remember the famous exaggeration, "Is this not great Babylon, which I have built by my mighty power as a royal residence and for the glory of my majesty?" (Dan 4:30). God's judgment was announced "while the words were still in the king's mouth" (Dan 4:31). We see excess with Herod in Acts 11:20–24 with an even more damaging outcome.

Excesses of self-esteem are not limited to those outside God's people. The description of Absalom in 2 Samuel 15:1–6 reeks of pride: "Absalom got himself a chariot and horses, and fifty men to run before him." This blatant self-promotion set the stage for rebellion. Diotrephes refused to acknowledge apostolic authority and opposed the faithful because he was a man "who likes to put himself first" (3 John 9). The church in Laodicea offers another stunning example. Their arrogant self-appraisal stood in stark contrast to the way that Jesus saw them (Rev 3:14–22). These are clear examples that "God opposes the proud but gives grace to the humble" (Jas 4:6, Prov 3:34).

A BIBLICAL UNDERSTANDING OF SELF-ESTEEM

We don't want to seem defensive or argumentative as we make the case for a biblical understanding of self-esteem. We acknowledge that some oppose such language on the most basic of levels: "Standard translations of the Bible do not even use the word self-esteem." We assert that the Bible can describe important concepts without using their names. For example, standard Bible translations do not use the words/phrases "trinity," "Christian counseling," "church building," or even "Bible."

Another common assertion: "Self-esteem is a concept invented by psychology—much of which is solidly secular if not anti-religious." We don't mean to offend with our language. If you prefer, you might think of value, self-worth, self-concept, or self-understanding. Our assertion is simple: the Bible teaches on this subject. While how we view ourselves is not the standard for discipleship, it certainly affects our walk with God.

Christian self-concept starts with Genesis 1:26–27. Humans, whether male or female, are made in the image, after the likeness, of God. Our value, dignity, capacity, and responsibility flow from that truth.

While God loves His entire creation, He views humans differently (Ps 8). From John 1:12–13 and 3:16–17 to Romans 5:1–11 and Romans 8, God loves, values, and wants to redeem us. Being loved by God is the ground of any human worth.

Several biblical passages acknowledge human worth and self-regard. From Matthew 7:12, "So whatever you wish that others would do to you, do also to them, for this is the Law and the Prophets." From Matthew 20:39, quoting Leviticus 19:18, "You shall love your neighbor as yourself." From Ephesians 5:25–30, "Husbands should love their wives as their own bodies" and "He who loves his wife loves himself." From Philippians 2:4, "Let each of you look not only to his own interests, but also to the interests of others."

Of course the major issue here is maintaining biblical perspective and biblical balance. Philippians 2:1–3 offers the perfect perspective. While we are loved by God and we're blessed by God to "look to" our own interests, we consciously and consistently put God and others ahead of self. The ESV phrases it beautifully: "but in humility count others more significant than yourself." We don't use our God-given uniqueness or self-esteem selfishly; we use what God gives to honor Him and bless others.

WHAT ARE THE MOST COMMON SELF-ESTEEM ISSUES?

We have no doubt that the most common and deadly issue with self-esteem is excess. We speak of pride—thinking too highly of self, thinking that we have some special standing where God's laws or the consequences of God's universe don't apply to us. Pride and selfishness bring untold pain to humanity. There is no greater wisdom than believing and applying Proverbs 1:7, 3:5–12, and 16:25. Micah 6:8, 1 Corinthians 10:12, and 1 Peter 5:5–7 stand forever true. God can't rule in a life that's led by pride.

Wisdom has long asserted that the devil doesn't care which ditch you're in; either way you're off the road. If the devil can't destroy through pride, he's happy to destroy our joy and service though false humility and low self-esteem. We see this often in hurting people. "If you knew what I had done, if you knew what I have been, you'd know that God can't save a person like me." But God forgave Abraham's doubt and lies. He forgave David's adultery and murder. He forgave Paul's persecution. He had the first gospel sermon after the resurrection preached in the city where Jesus was crucified and to the people who murdered Him (Acts 2).

For those who have become Christians, the stoutest form of this assertion is, "Yes, those examples might work for people who don't know better. I was a faithful, informed Christian when I sinned. I KNEW BETTER! There's no hope or grace for me." Again, this is demonstrably false. Jesus predicted Peter's denial to his face (Matt 26:33–35). Peter denied Jesus's prophecy, and then denied even knowing Him. And Jesus still forgave Peter. While we acknowledge the truth of Hebrews 6:4–8, we take heart in the fact that it isn't the whole of biblical teaching on the subject of willful sin.

Other Christians face spiritual self-esteem issues based on what some call "comparativitis": "I have no formal education. My talents are few. I don't have much money. What can a person like me do for Jesus anyway?" Think of the Parable of the Talents in Matthew 25. There is no difference in praise or reward for the five-talent and two-talent men. The one-talent man was in no way condemned because he had only one talent. His error was failing to use what he had. 2 Corinthians 8 offers a clinic on healthy versus unhealthy comparisons. The Macedonians were held up as an example to encourage the Corinthians, but all were reminded that we each give according to what we have. God doesn't judge according to what we don't possess (2 Cor 8:12).

We love the anti-false-comparison principle stated by Jesus in Mark 14:8: "She has done what she could." His logic is impeccable. There's no place for unrealistic expectations or false judgments.

One of the devil's big lies regarding Christian service is, "Go big or go home. If you can't do something great, then what you do won't matter." Fundamentally, this lie attacks God. It attacks faith. People who struggle with faith/self-esteem issues will need to be reminded of the power of little things in God's service. The principle is taught overtly in Luke 17:5–6: "The apostles said to the Lord, 'Increase our faith.' And the Lord said, 'If you had faith like a grain of mustard seed, you could say to this mulberry tree, Be uprooted and planted in the sea, and it would obey you.'" God can do amazingly more than we can imagine. If we act on the faith we have, that faith will grow. More importantly, God will be honored.

Can we offer non-miraculous biblical examples of the power and impact of seemingly small service? God used the overheard report of an enemy's dream to encourage Gideon before his greatest battle (Judg 7:13–14). Brethren saved Saul's (Paul's) life in Damascus by passing him through the wall in a large basket (Acts 9:23–25). God used a good word from Barnabas to get Saul the opportunity to worship with the brethren in Jerusalem (Acts 9:26–30). God used a report of a conversation overheard by a relative to save Paul's life (Acts 23:12ff). Through a quiet conversation, Aquila and Priscilla helped Apollos learn "the way of God more accurately" (Acts 18:26). Many of us have seen similar events where seemingly tiny actions contributed to notable victories. We know those victories would not have happened without the initial faithful effort.

WHY DOES THIS MATTER?

Why does it matter whether we believe we have any value to God? "You cited Luke 17:5 above talking about the value of even the smallest faith. Don't you remember the rest of the passage?" Jesus tells the story of a servant working hard and then fixing dinner for his master before he feeds himself. The attitude Jesus promotes is, "So you also, when you have done all that you were commanded, say, 'We are unprofitable servants; we have only done what was our duty'" (Luke 17:10).

The point is well taken. God is great, and we're not. It's His earth we stand on and His air we breathe; "in Him we live and move and have our being" (Acts 17:28). It is God who works in us "both to will and to do His good pleasure" (Phil 2:13).

Why do we offer help to those who question their worth to God? Why work to help people feel loved by God and wanted by God? Why do we help people recognize their ability to serve and bring glory to God?

The first answer is because that's what the Bible teaches leaders to do. God "desires all people to be saved and to come to the knowledge of the truth" (1 Tim 2:4). God desires that leaders in the church "equip the saints for the work of ministry, for building up the body of Christ" (Eph 4:12). God ordains that each member of the body contribute to stability, unity, and growth (Eph 4:11–16).

Recognizing that God loves us matters at the level of appreciation. There is no higher calling than to love God (Matt 22:37). Knowing that God loved us enough to send His Son to save us lifts our hearts and stirs our gratitude.

It fills us with joy and brings us the greatest peace (Phil 4:4–9).

Knowing that God values us matters at the level of motivation. 1 John 4:7–5:6 is outstanding as a whole, but we particularly note 4:11, "Beloved, if God so loved us, we also ought to love one another," and 5:3, "For this is the love of God, that we keep His commandments."

HOW TO HELP THOSE WHO DON'T YET FEEL VALUED BY GOD

Choose to be an instrument of God's love, realizing that, as we speak God's words in love, those words can "give grace to those who hear" (Eph 4:29). What a noble concept: We can be instruments of God's grace.

Be nice. Colossians 3:12–17 offers great wisdom. Sometimes people don't remember what we say as we try to help them. Often what they remember most vividly is that we were "compassionate hearers" who chose to be kind, caring, humble, and patient.

Listen to people's pain stories, but don't be content just to listen. Invite hurting people to follow the pattern of many Psalms. Pain and frustration are stated, the presence of evil is acknowledged, personal responsibility is accepted, and God is praised for His deliverance (Ps 6, 7, 10, 13). We recommend guided self-discovery. Help hurting people see this pattern and recognize its value. Offer support as people seek to live up to these insights.

Invite people to recognize and celebrate even the smallest victories. In this sin-damaged world, our vision is clouded. Additionally, victories in our service to God are often mixed. We seldom see the best possible outcome. But every victory granted by God is precious. Every victory that honors God matters. Think of Acts 16. We don't see Silas and Paul lamenting the false accusation, the beatings, or the imprisonment. We think of them joyous over new converts and the power of the gospel.

Clearly and kindly question bad thinking. Is your hurting friend condemning himself over outcomes that he did not want and could not control? Is your hurting friend judging herself for failing to reach expectations that God did not set? Is your hurting friend forgetting the fact that every person gets to choose his or her response to God's truth?

Be sweetly stubborn. Refuse to let people sell themselves short. 1 Corinthians 12 and Ephesians 4:11–16 teach that every member of the body counts. Every member has something to contribute. Every member is important to God. Refuse to let anyone tell you otherwise!

As you persist in helping, remember your limitations. Keep your expectations reasonable. Even with the best biblical help, some will face an ongoing battle to feel loved, forgiven, appreciated, and/or fit to serve. Let God's word and God's providence continue to work. Recommend passages and examples that encourage. Support ongoing service. Remind strugglers that it is NOT hypocritical to do (act, behave) better than you feel. In fact, acting better than we feel is evidence of faith, maturity and commitment. We believe the time-honored assertion: "It's easier to act (behave, serve) your way into better feelings than to feel your way into better actions."

1 John 3:19–20 may also help. In a context of enhancing assurance by putting our love into God-honoring action, John writes, "By this we shall know that we are of the truth and reassure our heart before him, for whenever our heart condemns us, God is greater than our heart, and He knows everything." For the faithful who struggle to feel assured or confident in Christ, this text offers a path to peace. Refuse to base your value or confidence on your feelings. Choose to trust God's word and God's grace more than your feelings. Choose to trust every word of Scripture and to let God be right in His judgment.

CHAPTER 20
THE POWER OF PREVENTION

We so wish we could remember where we first saw the church described as "a kingdom of right relationships." While incomplete, it's so helpful and so accurate. It fits Jesus's description of the first and second commandments (Matt 22:37–40). If we love God as fully as possible and love our neighbors as ourselves, all of life goes better. As church leaders, we value, model, support, and encourage godly relationships.

All church leaders who counsel are exposed to a darker view of life. Hurting people—often severely damaged and hurting people—seek our help. It can seem that everybody is in major pain. It can come to appear that most people live in crisis. While every human both experiences harm and sometimes hurts others, life isn't always as dark as our wearied perception.

PATHS TO DYSFUNCTION

We'd never deem ourselves wise enough to list, describe, and quantify every approach to emotional and relational pain. But there is value in remembering the most common paths. If we seek to decrease dysfunction, we need to know what we're trying to prevent.

At the top of the list is trying to be our own gods. We are not the source of power, truth, or righteousness (Job 38–42, Prov 16:2 & 25, Jer 10:23–24). We are not the standard by which all else is judged. We are not even close to all-knowing, and we don't really understand all that we think we know. There's major blessing in faithfully refusing to overestimate ourselves (Rom 12:3).

Frequent and painful is chasing the impossibility of trying to please everyone. Logically, people are exceedingly diverse. It's literally impossible to please everyone since people have stunningly different needs, wants, and agendas. One wants rain for his garden while another wants maximum sun for her picnic. One wants one-on-one time with one friend at a time while another wants a big gathering of family and friends.

Regrettable and self-punishing is failing to admit and learn from our errors. What's wrong, dumb, or less than the best is wrong, dumb, and less than the best even if we do it. We all err and sin (Rom 3:23). Failing to admit our failings is stunningly damaging. It demands wasting energy by trying to defend the indefensible. It makes us look bad and feel bad. It distances us from God and from people who can help us. It ensures that we fail to grow through our errors.

Classically foolish is choosing the wrong confidants

and advisers (Prov 13:20). Biblical examples include Hanun and his princes (2 Sam 10), Amnon and Jonadab (2 Sam 13:1–22), Rehoboam and the young men (1 Kgs 12), Ahab and Jezebel (1 Kgs 21), and Ahab with his false prophets (1 Kgs 22:1–7). All suffered ruin from listening to the wrong voices.

Ever more common is choosing entitlement. It's amazingly arrogant to think that the universe exists to meet my needs, that life should be as I prefer. To choose entitlement is to invite perpetual victimhood. Life will not always go as we prefer. Many of our expectations will go unfulfilled.

Tragically unwise is failing to differentiate true and false guilt. "Godly grief" that leads to repentance holds amazing power (2 Cor 7:10). But grinding sorrow over matters we did not cause and could not prevent causes only pain. Even the strongest feeling of sorrow holds no benefit unless it bears "fruit in keeping with repentance" (Matt 3:8).

Foolish to the core is choosing an unbiblical model of success or even meaningful existence. To the best of our knowledge, Abel never fathered a child, wrote a book, earned a degree, led a movement, or did any deed of renown. Yet he stands as an example of faithfulness (Heb 11:4). We don't even know the name of the widow who gave the two small coins, but we expect to see her in heaven (Mark 12:41–44). We know that God sees far better than we do (1 Sam 16:7, Rev 2:8–9). A life lived to God's glory never lacks success or meaning.

WHAT CAN CHURCH LEADERS DO TO PREVENT THESE PATHS TO PAIN?

If the church is in any sense a kingdom of right relationships, we want to minimize pain and dysfunction. We want to stop patterns and processes of neglect and abuse. We want to build love, joy, peace, trust, faith, and service. Part of doing this great work is accessing the power of prevention.

- Prevention of sin, self-will, and broken relationships is strategic on several levels.
- It follows the example of God (Gen 4:6–7, Deut 11:26–28).
- It invites people to forego the scars and residual effects that often accompany even sin that has been forgiven (2 Sam 12:7–14).
- It demonstrates the power of God's word to bless, guide, and protect (Ps 119:97–104, 2 Tim 3:16–17).
- It demonstrates biblical wisdom (Prov 22:3, 27:12).
- It demonstrates excellent stewardship. Often the resources—time, tears, effort, and expertise—required for prevention are far less than those needed for reclamation (Prov 18:19). At least two common-sense proverbs apply: "An ounce of prevention is worth a pound of cure," and "a stitch in time saves nine."

To practice effective prevention of spiritual and

emotional dysfunction, help people trust God. Teach people that God is good, gracious, merciful, and loving—even when life seems to say otherwise (Job 13:15, Rom 8:31–39, 2 Cor 4:7–16). The stories of Abraham, Joseph, Daniel, and Paul all powerfully document this truth. Please don't assume that hearers have already grasped this fact. Even if well-taught and well-received, humans have amazing capacity for forgetfulness (2 Pet 1:12–13).

Help people align their view of reality with God's. We are "sojourners and exiles" in this world (1 Pet 2:11–12). While we live here, we will have trouble (Job 14:1, John 16:1–4). The Bible offers no example of a godly person who experienced no challenges. In stark contrast, the religious world around us offers a powerful but errant counter-narrative asserting guaranteed health and wealth for all believers. It's a lie that many love to believe. It cannot stand the test of time.

Help people treat others right/lovingly always (Matt 5–7 & 25:31–40, Rom 12:3–21, 1 John 3:18). Through our personal examples, classes, sermons, and conversations, we must help people apply biblical principles of right conduct. Challenge what needs to be challenged; commend what merits commendation. Don't miss an opportunity to teach. Don't underestimate the power of modeling love and respect for others.

Help people face truth. While we can offer the gospel, we can't make anyone choose faith (Mark 10:17–22, Matt 23:37–39, John 1:11–13). To quote the great philosopher Clint Eastwood, "A man's got to know his limitations." Reality does not bend to our will. The gospel calls, but people can refuse it. Even though God is perfect and all-powerful, bad things still happen. And it remains far wiser to face pain and evil with God's help rather than without it.

Provide forums for shared wisdom and supportive healing. Consider a Bible class on "The Christian and Emotions." Begin with a pertinent text. Offer a few questions to promote thinking and application. Prepare to be amazed at how much people help one another in that setting. We have been stunningly impressed with the level of insight and impact that flows from such Bible-based discussion. See the suggested ten-week outline at the end of this chapter. Reminder: the lessons on fear, grief, and depression can be supplemented with material from chapters within this book. Also, if taught as a Bible class, some discussions are likely to expand beyond a single week.

Similar class series could be developed on a variety of subjects including:

- God's Guide to Getting Along with People
- A Biblical Course in Communication Skills
- A Biblical Plan for Staying Healthy and Whole
- Biblical Keys to Problem Solving
- Keys to Sound Thinking in a Mixed-Up World

Within the church setting, forums for shared wisdom and supportive healing can be fostered by sermons designed to promote biblical well-being. Seminars focused on prevention can both bless church members and serve as a contact point for evangelistic outreach. Sharing links to online resources and adding helpful books to the church library can also enhance the "prevention menu." Warning: If a congregation chooses to emphasize prevention and healing, the church's counseling load will increase at least in the short run. It's amazing how people respond when they see us making effort to help them. Please choose to view this increased workload as both a blessing and an indicator that important needs are being met.

Support those who "get up and go on" with God. Even very strong people get knocked down by life. Think of David in Psalm 51. Think of Elijah in 1 Kings 19. Think of Peter's denial (Matt 26:31–35 & 69–75). Think of Barnabas (Gal 2:13). When people hit rough patches, they need such examples. They need to be reminded that God is fiercely loyal and loving.

We must stay spiritually healthy ourselves. If people hear us say one thing but model another, they will believe their eyes! Virtually everyone hates hypocrisy (Matt 23:1–14). Oppositely, we're blessed to love the consistency and congruence of Jesus. Luke emphasized his attention on "all that Jesus began to do and teach" (Acts 1:1). His actions and teachings always corresponded; they always honored God (John 8:29). May the same be true of us!

CONCLUSION

Within the realm of church leadership and pastoral counseling, prevention is non-glamorous. It almost never brings "ah ha" moments when people tell us, "Thank you. This has helped me so much! I feel like I can move forward with God now."

While the benefits of preventing unhealthy living will be quieter and less obvious, God will not let them remain invisible. In a sense, it's like parenting. We teach and model "the discipline and instruction of the Lord" without seeing daily results or rewards (Eph 6:4). But eventually, we're blessed to learn that God's truth has changed hearts to be like Jesus (Eph 4:11–16, Prov 23:24). Sweet!

THE CHRISTIAN AND EMOTIONS

1. A biblical view of emotion.

   - Genesis 1:26–27 & 3:22, Psalm 8:4–5, Proverbs 16:2 & 25.
   - Are emotions more of a necessary evil or a blessed part of being human? Explain.
   - Are emotions a safe guide for our behavior?
   - To what degree and in what ways does Scripture present the emotions of Jesus? What should that teach us?
   - Without emotion, life would be _____.
   - If I live by my emotions, life will be _____.

2. Fear.

   - Matthew 10:16–31 and 14:22–33.
   - In what ways can fear be a helpful emotion?
   - In what ways can fear be harmful or destructive?

- Is it desirable for us to become fearless?
- Is it possible for us to become fearless?
- Is there a difference between feeling fearful and acting fearful? Explain.

3. Worry.

- Matthew 6:25–34.
- What are the basic differences between healthy concern and unhealthy worry?
- Why do so many Christians continue to be plagued by worry?
- What actions would you recommend to a person who wants to overcome worry?
- Is worry really as harmful as some seem to believe? In what ways can worry harm us?

4. Happiness.

- Philippians 1–4. Note the words "joy," "rejoice," and "content."
- How could a man who was often persecuted and imprisoned write Philippians 4:4?
- In what ways do people seek happiness? How often and at what level do they succeed?
- What do Psalm 144:15 & 146:5 and John 13:13–17 tell us about happiness?
- Is happiness an emotional state or feeling, or is biblical happiness something more (Acts 5:41, Hebrews 10:14 &12:2, 1 Peter 4:12–14)?

5. Hate and Anger.

- Esther 1–10, John 2:13–17, Luke 1:33–34 with 1 Peter 2:23, Ephesians 4:26.
- What's the difference between hate and anger? Do these differences matter?
- Is hatred rational? Consider Haman's hatred of Mordecai.
- In that it is possible to be angry without sinning, what keeps anger from moving to sin?
- What are the major sources of anger for most people?

6. Love.

- Ruth 1:1–18, Matthew 5:43–44, 1 Corinthians 13.
- Is the love described in Matthew 5 and 1 Corinthians 13 an emotion? Can it be emotionless? If it's not just an emotion, what is it?
- To what degree is love a choice? How do we choose to love the people whom we love?
- What are the major flaws in the world's concept of love?

7. Guilt.

- 2 Samuel 11–12 with Psalms 32 and 51, Matthew 26:73–27:5, 2 Corinthians 7:8–9.
- What are the major differences between "godly sorrow" (spiritually beneficial guilt, 2

Corinthians 7:10) and worldly sorrow (detrimental guilt)?
- Why do some have such a strong tendency to feel guilty while others lack that tendency? What are the dangers of each tendency?
- What are the major causes of guilt for Christians?
- Why do some Christians continue to feel guilty even after repentance and confession of sin?

8. Depression.

- 1 Kings 19, 2 Corinthians 4:7–18.
- Agree or disagree and explain. "Everybody gets depressed now and then; it's really no big deal."
- Why is depression so common in our society?
- What can we do to minimize episodes of depression? Can depression be prevented?
- What can we do to help a depressed friend?

9. Envy and Jealousy.

- 1 Samuel 18:1–9, Matthew 27:1–2 & 17–18, 1 Corinthians 3:1–3.
- What's the difference between envy and jealousy?
- In what ways do envy and jealousy harm individuals? Families? Churches?
- Agree or disagree and explain: "A little jealousy is good for a relationship."

- What causes a person to become envious/jealous?
- How can a person battle/overcome envy/jealousy?

10. Grief.

- 2 Samuel 1, Lamentations 1–5.
- Is there really any way to prepare for grief?
- Is it beneficial to attempt to prepare?
- What emotions are most commonly associated with grief? Why?
- To what degree do we have control of our emotions during grief?
- What can we do to help those we love endure and grow through their grief?

CHAPTER 21
TAKING SUFFICIENT CARE OF OURSELVES
THE ART OF GOOD BOUNDARIES

"Good morning, ladies and gentlemen. Welcome aboard American flight AA2921 to Dallas/Fort Worth. Thank you for your attention while important safety information is reviewed. In preparation for departure . . . blah, blah, blah . . . Fasten your seatbelts . . . approved flotation . . .blah, blah . . . Locate the exit . . . If needed, oxygen masks will be released overhead. To start the flow . . . blah . . . Place the mask over your nose and mouth . . . **Be sure to secure your own mask before assisting others.**" *What? Don't put the mask on my child first? Don't help my elderly friend before getting my own oxygen? But that's not what Christians do! We put the needs of others ahead of our own, right? What would Jesus do?* I once heard a flight attendant discussing this self-first instruction with a passenger. She said, "I might could help you, but then I would pass out without oxygen and what would happen to the others that need my help? The best chance of a good outcome for the greatest number of people is for the helpers to be able to help."

Is that what Jesus would do? Yes. Jesus recognized the need to care for himself and for those around him to take care of themselves as well. He set priorities that included the purpose of his mission, the needs of the people, the attitudes of those around him, and time management. Jesus also addressed the needs for a support system, rest, food, quiet-time alone with God, prayer, and communicating with others (Matt 4:23–25, 14:1–14, & 14:15–21; Mark 6:7–13, 6:30–32, & 14:7; Luke 4:1–2, 14–15, 4:42–44, 5:16, 6:12–13, 10:1–2, 19:10, & 22:39–44).

I want to take a closer look at a time when we see Jesus engaging in "self-care" and encouraging his apostles to do the same. In Mark 6 we find Jesus sending out the Twelve, two-by-two, in keeping with the need to have a partner or a support system. He also instructed them to work with people who were receptive, but to "shake off the dust that is on your feet" (Mark 6:11) of those who would not listen. Jesus does not ask us to persist in unproductive helping. Continuing in Mark 6, we have the account of the death of John the Baptist, Jesus's cousin and forerunner. The death of John had to be a great loss to Jesus personally and to several of Jesus's disciples who had been followers of John.

The next information shared after John's death tells of the apostles' return to Jesus after their teaching and preaching tour. Jesus gave them the opportunity to tell him what had happened in their travels. He immediately advised them to

"Come away by yourselves to a desolate place to rest a while." For many were coming and going and they had no leisure even to eat. And they went away in the boat to a desolate place by themselves (Mark 6:30–32).

Jesus realized the need for debriefing, boundaries, nutrition, and rest. Jesus listened as the apostles told him what had happened. I think we can assume that he already knew all that had happened, but he knew they needed to talk about it. He encouraged them to put some space—a boundary—between themselves and the crowds of people. He wanted them to have ample opportunity to eat and rest.

There are other times recorded when Jesus was not engaged in teaching or healing. In the accounts in Matthew 8, Mark 4, and Luke 8, Jesus was so tired he was sleeping through a storm while traveling by boat on the Sea of Galilee. We do not know if this was due to physical, emotional, or spiritual fatigue—or if his sleeping was a combination of causes. On other occasions Jesus took the apostles and retreated from the crowds up to Caesarea Philippi. Sometimes he wanted to be completely alone; sometimes with his inner circle of Peter, James, and John. If Jesus needed to engage in self-care and encouraged his followers to do so, we need to consider what we too can do to avoid the pitfall of running on empty. When we are involved in ministry, we can become vulnerable to making mistakes, lapses of judgment, and even the potential of burnout. We also put ourselves at risk for physical illness and emotional or psychological distress. Above all, the effects of burnout even include putting ourselves at risk spiritually.

What is burnout? What should we be looking for in our fellow laborers and ourselves? Burnout, compassion fatigue, and vicarious depression are all terms for similar conditions. Often there are warning signs that are noticeable; but also it is possible that due to guilt, embarrassment, or fear an individual would cover-up these warning signs. A person could experience any or all of the following indicators:

1. Lack of motivation. Lack of motivation is characterized by finding ourselves dreading engaging in ministry activities or not feeling the passion or urge to help others.

2. Loss of hope. When we lose hope, we have inwardly given up. We doubt that people can change or want to change, that the church can grow, or that even with God's guidance our efforts can make a difference.

3. Lack of energy. People drain the life out of us. Even after a good night's sleep or a weekend away with our families, we have no energy. In fact, after doing things that used to revive us, we find ourselves more tired than before.

4. Loss of joy. Nothing seems fun or funny anymore. People and activities we have enjoyed in the past no longer bring us pleasure. We find ourselves repulsed by people who are having fun. We may seek other sources of joy—alcohol, drugs, pornography, and/or video games.

5. Loss of focus. Loss of focus impacts our productivity. It takes longer to get tasks accomplished, or we move from one activity to another without completing anything. We may feel that the activities are futile or they may seem overwhelming.

6. Feeling alone. We feel isolated and misunderstood. We don't talk to anybody about our feelings, and we

choose to spend time alone rather than with those who could help.

7. *Experiencing resentment and bitterness.* We become cynical and no longer see the potential for good that lies in each individual. We do not see good in ourselves as well. We don't enjoy being with others, which leads us to avoid interaction.[1, 2]

When considering the consequences of burnout, it is evident that it is something we need to avoid. As with so many things in life, avoiding or preventing burnout doesn't just happen. Intentional, purposeful action is required to be successful in keeping ourselves healthy. Many things can be implemented, and each plan for self-care needs to be individualized. What works for one person may not work for anyone else. Let's identify some possibilities that could be helpful.

1. Maintain a healthy perspective. Perspective on what? Everything. Remember, we are in the role of helper. We cannot control the behavior of others, nor the choices they make. Our role is to listen, care, encourage and teach. Ultimately our goal as a counseling church leader is to "help people find peace with God, peace with others, and peace with themselves."[3] Success in Christian counseling comes when the client acknowledges God, behaves in ways consistent with the teachings of Jesus, and allows the Holy Spirit, the comforter, to guide his or her life. Maintaining a healthy perspective can include taking care of ourselves and recognizing our limitations. We can only do what we can, and then get out of the way and allow God to do his work. Too many church leaders "burnout because they give out."[4]

2. Step back when you need to shift priorities. As was

discussed earlier, Jesus would take a step back from ministry to rest and regroup. He would pray to his heavenly Father and spend time with his earthly support system. We need to do the same. Taking time for ourselves is not to be confused with being self-centered. In *Jesus, the Greatest Therapist Who Ever Lived*, Mark Baker states, "The centered self is not self-centered."[5] When Jesus's followers rebuked the woman for anointing his feet and failing to care for the poor, Jesus praises her action and points out "you always have the poor with you." I think we could say as church leaders, "We will always have the poor, the lonely, the discouraged" and many other needs, but sometimes it is right to take time for ourselves. Helping others is a never-ending job. There will never be a time when all the needs of every member of the congregation have been met. If we wait until that problem-free time comes to practice self-care, it will never happen.

3. Stay connected to healthy people. Not only do people need us, we need people. Yes, even if we are introverts. Before we get burned out and wish people would just go away, we should take time to connect to people whom we enjoy being around. Seek out those who encourage and energize us, but who also will confront us and hold us accountable. We need people in our lives with whom our relationship is a pleasure. We hope there are people who watch our backs. If not, we need to make efforts to develop that type of relationship. Then we need to be willing to welcome help. Ours friends may realize something is wrong in our lives before we do. They may be fellow church leaders, or they may be people not connected to our congregation, but they are people who are our friends, our support system. Jesus had them, twelve of them and then within that group a smaller sub-group. We need those people too, and we need to spend time with them. Make sure it happens. Be intentional.

4. *Have a healthy lifestyle.* We need to take care of physical health through getting proper amounts of rest, eating a balanced diet, and exercising. We know to do those things, but they are easily neglected. Be intentional.

5. *Get a hobby.* Several years ago I (Rosemary) attended a workshop designed to help counselors cope with stress. I had heard all the things I shared in items 1–4. These were things I already knew, but then the presenter told us we needed to get a hobby. Of course we all thought, "I don't have time for a hobby!" As I listened, I realized the presenter had some very good points about the importance of having a hobby. I may not remember all I was taught that day, but here are the takeaways for me:

- Get a hobby—learn a new skill or enhance an existing skill. Find an activity to enjoy.
- Select a hobby that allows obvious accomplishments—an activity where a project can be completed. For example you might try woodworking, knitting (my choice), or gardening. Because counseling and helping others is a never-ending task, it is important to have a hobby where we can see a finished product. It will give a sense of accomplishment and closure, which are both positive emotions.

- Interact with others who enjoy the same or a similar hobby. Positive interaction with others can be stimulating and contribute to positive experiences of being helped and helping others.
- Hobbies help to mitigate the effects of chronic stress and thereby help prevent burnout. It gives us something to look forward to and provides an outlet after a long day or a difficult counseling session.
- A completed project can lead to positive feedback from others. Other people will compliment our work or appreciate what we have accomplished. These interactions lead to improved self-esteem.

6. *Stay spiritually healthy enough to help.* We must remain vigilant in assessing our spiritual well-being. We should ask ourselves the following:

- Am I still doing what God says to do? (Matt 7:21–23)
- Am I still praying, growing, and learning? (2 Pet 1, Gal 5:22–26)
- Am I loving others with the love of the Lord? (Matt 22:36–40)
- Am I still trusting and relying on God? Am I trusting myself too much? (Proverbs 3:5–8)

Other ongoing healthy practices include prayer, Bible study, worship, confession, repentance, loving service, forgiving others, accepting God's forgiveness, and choosing joy in God's blessings.

What an honor it is to serve God by serving others! The paradox of least and greatest, servant and leader is stunningly evident in counsel from church leaders. Many ministry activities have very visible results: the number of baptisms, attendance, how many meals were fed or homeless housed, but not counseling. An intricate part of the counseling process is the confidentiality involved in the relationship. What happens in counseling will not be known by others, and very often we do not know the effectiveness of our efforts for weeks, months, years, or maybe ever. Our success is measured in changed lives and in improved relationships and within the hearts of our clients. Success in counseling is not information to be published on social media, in the church bulletin nor celebrated in an announcement from the pulpit. Success is found when we see a family sitting together during worship, a teenager graduating from high school, an elderly church member transitioning peacefully into eternity. Our goal is to be servants of God and to help others do the same without anyone even noticing.

ENDNOTES

[1.] Claybury/One Another Ministries, *The Elijah-Decision: When Stress Sucks Away Your Will to Go On*, christian-leadership.org/stress-mini-course-mk-2/the-elijah-decision-when-stress-sucks-away-your-will-to-go-on/.

[2.] Aaron Buer, *5 Warning Signs of Ministry Burnout*, https://www.breezechms.com/blog/5-warning-signs-of-ministry-burnout.

3. Gary Collins. *Christian Counseling: A Comprehensive Guide* (Nashville: Thomas Nelson, 2006), 589.
4. Collins, *Christian Counseling*, 588.
5. Mark Baker, *Jesus, The Greatest Therapist Who Ever Lived*, (New York: HarperOne, 2007), 284.

RECOMMENDED RESOURCES

The following older works provide excellent basic resources for people-helping. Each is to be read advisedly, using the fish/bones principle with the Bible as our ultimate guide.

Bramson, Robert M. *Coping with Difficult People.* Garden City, NY: Anchor Press/Doubleday, 1981.

Collins, Gary. *How to Be a People Helper: You Can Help the Others in Your Life.* Santa Ana, CA; Vision House Publishers, 1979.

McGinnis, Alan L. *The Friendship Factor: How to Get Closer to the People You Care For.* Minneapolis: Augsburg Publishing House, 1979.

_____. *Bringing Out the Best in People: How to Enjoy Helping Others Excel.* Minneapolis: Augsburg Publishing House, 1985.

The books below offer broader and advanced help for effective counseling.

Benner, David G. *Strategic Pastoral Counseling: A Short-Term Structured Model.* 2nd ed. Grand Rapids, MI: Baker Academic, 2003.

Collins, Gary R. *Christian Counseling: A Comprehensive Guide.* 3rd ed. Nashville: Thomas Nelson, 2007.

Flatt, Bill. *Restoring My Soul: The Pursuit of Spiritual Resilience.* Nashville, Gospel Advocate, 2001.

Hamblen, Betty. *Emotional Fitness: A Counselor's Perspective.* Bloomington, IN: Inspiring Voices, 2012.

Hetzendorfer, Ruth. *Pastoral Counseling Handbook: A Guide for Helping the Hurting.* Kansas City: Beacon Hill Press, 2009.

Johnson, W. Brad, and William L. Johnson. *The Minister's Guide to Psychological Disorders and Treatments.* 2nd ed. New York: Routledge Publishing, 2014.

Kollar, Charles A. *Solution-Focused Pastoral Counseling: An Effective Short-Term Approach for Getting People Back on Track.* Updated and expanded. Grand Rapids, MI: Zondervan, 2011.

Kottler, Jeffrey. *The Nuts and Bolts of Helping.* Boston: Allyn and Bacon, 2000.

Shanotto, Elisabeth A. Nesbitt, Heather D. Gringrich, and Fred C. Gringrich. *Skills for Effective Counseling: A Faith-Based Integration.* Downers Grove, IL: InterVarsity Press, 2016.

Thomas, John C. *Counseling Techniques: A Comprehensive Guide for Christian Counselors.* Grand Rapids, MI: Zondervan, 2018.

Watson, Jeffrey. *Biblical Counseling for Today: A Handbook for Those Who Counsel from Scripture.* Nashville: Word, 2000.

WORKS CITED

The American Association of Christian Counselors. *Code of Ethics.* http://www.aacc.net.

American Psychiatric Association. *Diagnostic and Statistical Manual of Mental Disorders.* 5th ed. *DSM-5.* Washington, D.C.: American Psychiatric Association, 2013.

Baker, Mark W. *Jesus, The Greatest Therapist Who Ever Lived.* New York: HarperOne, 2007.

Barrett, Lisa F., Michael Lewis, and Jeanne H. M. Haviland-Jones, eds. *Handbook of Emotions.* New York: Guilford Press, 2016.

Beck, A.T., A. John Rush, Brian E. Shaw, and Gary Emery. *Cognitive Therapy of Depression.* New York: Guilford, 1979.

Bramson, Robert M. *Coping with Difficult People.* Garden City, NY: Anchor Press/Doubleday, 1981.

Brown, Jessica. *Making Room at the Well: Mental Health and the Church.* Valley Forge, PA: Judson Press, 2020.

Buer, Aaron. *5 Warning Signs of Ministry Burnout.* https://www.breezechms.com/blog/5-warning-signs-of-ministry-burnout.

Centers for Disease Control and Prevention, NCHS Data Brief No. 362, April 2020. http://www.cdc.gov.

Chapman, Gary. *The Five Languages of Love: How to Express Heartfelt Commitment to Your Mate.* Chicago: Northfield Publishers, 1992.

Claybury/One Another Ministries. *The Elijah-Decision: When Stress Sucks Away Your Will to Go On.* christian-leadership.org/stress-mini-course-mk-2/the-elijah-decision-when-stress-sucks-away-your-will-to-go-on/.

Clinton, Tim. *The Struggle Is Real: How to Care for Mental and Relational Health Issues in the Church.* Bloomington, IN: Author Solutions, 2017.

Cloud, Henry, and John Townsend. *Boundaries: When to Say Yes, When to Say No to Take Control of Your Life.* Grand Rapids: Zondervan, 1992.

Collins, Gary. *Christian Counseling: A Comprehensive Guide.* Rev. ed. Dallas: Word Publishing, 1988.

Collins, Gary. *Christian Counseling: A Comprehensive Guide.* Nashville: Thomas Nelson, 2006.

Cook, Christopher C. H. *The Bible and Mental Health: Towards a Biblical Theology of Mental Health.* Louisville: Westminster John Knox Press, 2020.

Egan, Gerard, and Robert Reese. *The Skilled Helper: A Problem-Management & Opportunity-Development Approach to Helping.* Boston: Cengage, 2019.

Evans, Patricia. *The Verbally Abusive Relationship: How to Recognize It and How to Respond.* 2nd ed. Holbrook, MA: Adams Media Corp, 1996.

Farberow, N.L. and E.S. Shneidman, eds. *The Cry for Help.* New York: McGraw-Hill, 1965.

Gross, James J., ed. *Handbook of Emotional Regulation.* New York: Guilford Press, 2014.

Grcevich, Stephen. *Mental Health and the Church: A Ministry Handbook for Including Children and Adults with ADHD, Anxiety Mood Disorders, and Other Common Mental Health Conditions.* Grand Rapids: Zondervan, 2017.

Groves, J. Alasdair, and Winston T. Smith. *Untangling Emotions.* Wheaton, IL: Crossway, 2019.

Harley, Jr., Willard F. *His Needs, Her Needs: Building an Affair-Proof Marriage.* Fifteenth Anniversary Edition. Grand Rapids: Fleming H. Revell, 2001.

Kenney-Moore, Eileen, and Jeannie C. Watson. *Expressing Emotion: Myths, Realities, and Therapeutic Strategies.* New York: Guilford Press, 1999.

Kubler-Ross, Elizabeth. *On Death and Dying: What the Dying Have to Teach Doctors, Nurses, Clergy, and Their Own Families.* New York: Simon & Schuster, 1969.

Lewis, C.S. *The Problem of Pain.* United Kingdom: The Centenary Press, 1940. Current edition published by HarperCollins.

Meier, Paul. *Don't Let Jerks Get the Best of You: Advice for Dealing with Difficult People.* Nashville: Thomas Nelson, 1991.

Meier, Scott T., and Susan R. Davis. *The Elements of Counseling.* 6th ed. Pacific Grove, CA: Thomson Brooks/Cole, 2008.

National Institute of Mental Health. *Depression: Risk Factors.* http://www.nimh.nih.gov.

National Institute of Mental Health. *Mental Health Information: Statistics.* http://www.nimh.nih.gov.

Parrott, Les. *High Maintenance Relationships: How to Handle Impossible People*. Wheaton, IL: Tyndale House, 1996.

Rumsfeld, Donald.U.S. Department of Defense news briefing, (February 12, 2002).

Saarni, Carolyn. *The Development of Emotional Competence*. New York: Guilford Press, 1999.

Stafford, Matthew S. *Grace for the Afflicted: A Clinical and Biblical Perspective on Mental Illness*. Downers Grove, IL: InterVarsity Press, 2017.

Substance Abuse and Mental Health Services Association. *Help Prevent Suicide*. 10/7/2020. http://www.SAMHSA.gov.

Suicide and Crisis Center of North Texas. "*Warning signs of suicide.*" https://www.sccenter.org/facts-and-resources/warning-signs/

SCRIPTURE INDEX

Old Testament
Genesis

Reference	Pages
1:1	31
1:26	33
1:26–27	27, 178, 190, 218, 236, 251
1:31	202
2:18	33, 171, 221, 232
2:21–24	221
2:24	210
2:26–27	77
3	52, 82, 232
3–4	28
3:6	219
3:9ff	13
3:9–17	62
3:12	219
3:15	13
3:21	232
3:22	251
3:26–27	85
4	82, 130
4:1	221, 232
4:3–7	75
4:4–5	197
4:5	14, 126
4:6	14
4:6–7	247
4:6–8	11
4:7	15
4:8	14, 15, 219
6	28
6:5	28, 86
12:7–8	195
12:10–20	148
12:10–29	219
13:4	195
13:18	195
16:6–14	75
18:17–19	175
18:18–19	221
18:19	6
18:22–33	63
20:1–18	148, 219
21:14–21	75
21:17	63
26:6–11	148
37	86
37:2	162
37:3	162
37:12–32	162
37:34	162
37:35	162, 192
39	86
45:25–28	162

Exodus

Reference	Pages
1:15–22	228
2:24	63
3	102
3:7	63, 75–76
4	102

4:10–13	4	2:17ff	6
4:14	125	3	6
5:1–2	234	**1 Samuel**	
18:13–27	6	1	162
18:17	6	1:4	195
19:16	148	1:6	163
20:15–16	197	1:8	163
22:27	85	1:9ff	163
25:3–4	125	2:1–10	163
32	7	14:1–14	152
32:10	125	15	51
32:13	125	16:7	25, 246
32:14	125	17:33–37	19
32:32	138	18	86
34:6	86	18:1	181
34:29–35	7	18:1–4	232
Leviticus		18:1–9	254
19:18	236	20:24–34	126
Numbers		21:10–15	112, 148
11:1	85	**2 Samuel**	
11:10	85	1	255
11:33	85	1:25–26	181
13	192	7	187
14:18	86	10	246
Deuteronomy		11–12	233, 253
6:1–9	28, 175	12	18, 216
6:4–9	221	12:1–6	215
10:12–13	26	12:7	215
11:26–28	247	12:7–12	19, 164
13:1–5	7	12:7–14	247
15:19–21	197	13:1	87
32:36	85	13:1–6	7
Joshua		13:1–20	218
1:1–9	7	13:1–22	246
14:6–15	192	13:15	87
24:1–31	192	13:21	164
24:14ff	29	13:23–29	163
Judges		15:1–6	163, 235
4:4–9	152	16	30, 86
6:12	186	16:11–12	30
7:13–14	239	16:20–23	163
Ruth		18:5	163
1:1–18	253	18:33	164
1:16–17	181, 232	19	164

22:7	63	31:5–7	234
1 Kings		38–42	245
11:1–5	7	38:1–42:6	17
12	246	40:3–5	17
19	19, 216, 250, 254	42:1–6	17
		Psalms	
19:4–5a	137	6	241
19:9	216	7	241
19:10	172	8	190, 218, 236
19:13	216	8:4–5	251
21	219, 233, 246	8:5–6	27
21:1–16	7	10	241
22:1–7	246	13	241
2 Kings		19	202
13:24	85	19:1	32
Nehemiah		23	19, 152
13:23–37	129	24:1	31
Esther		25:16	171–172
1–10	253	27:3	147, 156
4:13–17	148	32	253
4:14	50	36:4	86
Job		43	138
1–2	17	51	197, 250, 253
1:1–5	6	55:1–8	148
1:5	195	69	138
1:6–2:7	209	78:70–72	19
1:8	16	79:13	19
1:20	138	81:8	61
1:22	16	81:11	61
2:9	138	88	138
2:11–13	17, 82, 203	95:6–7	19
2:13	138	100:3	19
3:11	138	102	138
3:26	138	102:6–7	172
4:7	17	103	201
4:7–9	209	103:13	85
4:7–10	218	118:6	147
7:20–21	209	119	201
8:1–7	218	119:11	201
10:1	138	119:15–16	201
11:1–6	218	119:97	201
13:15	17, 248	119:97–104	247
14:1	248	119:105–112	107
30:15–17	138	119:111–112	201–202

SCRIPTURE INDEX

119:148	202	16:25	26, 237, 245, 251
127:3–5	221	16:27–30	218
135:14	85	16:32	56, 127, 196
136	201	17:27–28	196, 203
139	201	18:9	196
139:1–4	62	18:13	196, 203, 210
139:23–24	25, 205, 234	18:19	228, 247
144:15	252	18:22	221
145:8–21	210	18:24	176
146:5	252	19:11	127, 196
Proverbs		19:14	221
1:7	237	19:19	126
1:8–9	61	19:24	196
1:10–19	218	20:4	196
1:22	61	20:11	26, 54, 56
3:3		21:2	23, 26, 205
3:5–8	234, 263	21:5	196
3:5–12	237	22:3	247
3:34	235	22:6	29
4		22:13	196
6:6–11	196	22:24–25	127–128, 179, 218
8:32–36	61	23:4–5	110
10:4–5	196	23:20–21	218
10:19	61–62, 203	23:24	251
10:23	196	24:1	218
12:4	221	24:30–34	196
12:5–6	218	25:8–10	196
12:26	218	25:11	169
12:27	196	25:11–12	176, 191, 203, 215
13:4	196	25:25	176
13:18	196	25:27	60
13:20	218, 246	25:28	56, 196
14:17	196	26:4–5	229
14:29	126–127, 196	26:12	23
15:1	133	26:13–16	196
15:1–2	203	27:2	60
15:5	196	27:12	247
15:19	196	27:21–22	218
15:18	126	29:11	2, 196, 203, 213
15:31–33	196	29:15	221
16:2	245, 251		
16:18	102		
16:24	196		

29:20	196	1:2	165
29:22	126	1:3	165
30:7–9	110	1:7	165
30:24–31	202	2:11–13	165
31		2:17–19	165
31:10–31	221	3:1–18	165
Ecclesiastes		3:22–24	166
3:7	2, 203	3:25–27	166
4:9–11	33	3:31–33	166
4:9–12	108, 156	**Ezekiel**	
7:9	126, 196	3:6–7	184
Isaiah		18	29, 56, 210, 221
1	20		
1:1–20	76	18:20	29
1:2	20	18:30	29
1:3	20	27:3	235
1:4	20	28:2	235
1:5	21	33	16, 29
1:5–9	20	33:11	21
1:10–15	20	37	193
1:11–15	21	**Daniel**	
1:16–17	20–21	2:17–18	195
1:18–20	20	3:8–23	228
9:6	128	3:16–18	103, 148
53:5	75	4:30	235
55:7	85	4:31	235
55:8–9	216	6:10	195
Jeremiah		7:3	76
1:10–2:37	165	7:20ff	76
1:19	184	9	76
5:14–17	165	9:3–27	195
5:18–19	165	**Jonah**	
10:23–24	26, 245	4:3	138
17:9	23	4:9	138
20:14	138	**Micah**	
20:18	138	2:1	86
23	7	6:8	29, 214, 229, 237
23:9–40	219		
29:1–23	219	**Nahum**	
44:16	184	1:3	127
Lamentations		**Habakkuk**	
1	76	2:3	103
1–5	255	**Malachi**	
1:1	165	1:7–9	197

SCRIPTURE INDEX

2:16	210	9:36	75, 85
New Testament		10:16–31	251
		10:25–33	152
Matthew		10:28	152
3:8	197, 246	10:42	190
3:14	74	11:15	61
4:6	157	12:14	86
4:23–25	257	12:24	86
5	253	12:36	107
5–7	248	13	228
5:9	90, 156, 229	13:9	61
5:13–16	60, 202	13:43	61
5:16	190	14:1–14	257
5:21–26	109–110	14:14	75, 85
5:22	127	14:15–21	257
5:23–24	153, 155	14:22–33	251
5:38–42	203	15:1–2	86
5:43–44	253	15:12	86, 228
5:43–48	90, 176, 203	15:28	189
6:1	234	15:32	85
6:1–18	60	15:53	75
6:5	234	16:5–12	218
6:16	234	16:17	189
6:19–21	32	16:21–23	219
6:25–34	120, 252	17:24–27	227
7:1–4	219	18	135
7:1–5	25, 234	18:15	155
7:7	207	18:15–17	155
7:12	59, 64, 83,	18:15–20	110, 135
96, 102, 123, 176, 203,		18:19	207
215, 236		19:4–6	210
7:15	219	19:26	193
7:21	26	20:25–28	202
7:21–23	233, 263	20:28	1, 180, 232
7:28–29	181	20:34	75
8	74, 258	20:39	236
8:7	74	21:12–16	86
8:10–13	189	21:45–46	86
8:16–17	74	22:30	231
8:28–34	114	22:34–40	10, 87
9:2	189	22:36–40	263
9:3	86	22:37	75, 197, 240
9:22	189	22:37–40	244
9:34	86	23:1–14	250

23:2–3	26	9:14–29	114, 157
23:5–12	200	9:24	157
23:14–15	200	9:36	147, 156
23:15	86	10:17–22	16, 214, 248
23:23–24	200	12:37	181
23:37	75	12:41–44	232, 246
23:37–39	11, 165, 248	12:42	190
25	102, 238	14:3–9	190, 232
25:14–30	149	14:7	257
25:31–40	248	14:8	238
25:34–40	76	14:34–36	138
25:39–40	145	15:11–15	219
26	54	**Luke**	
26:3–4	86	1:25–38	202
26:31–35	250	1:33–34	253
26:33–35	148, 238	2:37	195
26:36–38	82	2:41–52	73
26:36–39	208	2:52	93
26:36–42	203	4:1–2	257
26:36–46	96	4:14–15	257
26:37–38	172	4:16	195
26:38	138	4:42–44	257
26:57–68	86	5:16	257
26:69–75	148, 250	6:12–13	257
26:73–27:5	253	7:9	25
27:1–2	254	7:13	85
27:3–5	138	7:36–50	25
27:17–18	254	8	258
27:20–25	86	8:18	61
28:18–20	27	9:23–24	28
Mark		9:23–26	233
1:35	101, 195, 199	10	27, 232
3:1–5	125	10:1	33
3:5	85	10:1–2	257
3:14	172	10:25ff	79
3:20–21	112	10:25–37	59
4	258	10:27	82
4:24	61	11:1	198
6	257	11:9	54
6:7	33, 191	12:15	110
6:7–13	257	13:1–5	197
6:11	257	17:5	240
6:30–32	257–258	17:5–6	157, 239
6:31	101	17:5–10	22

17:10	240
18:1	193
18:9–14	25
18:11	78
19:9	25
19:10	107, 257
21:3	25
22:31–32	157
22:39–44	257
22:44	138
22:55–62	138
23:34	82, 135

John

1:11–13	190, 248
1:12–13	236
2:13–17	125, 129, 253
3:16	27, 87, 178, 218
3:16–17	21, 190, 202, 236
4:1–26	65
4:23–24	190
4:39	66
5:31–47	25
7:13	149
7:24	219
8:10–11	216
8:11	82
8:29	26, 250
8:31–32	212
8:32	81
8:37–38	107
8:44	197
9:1–3	209
9:22	149
10:10	1, 190
10:20	112
11:16	204
11:35	75
12:42–43	149
13:13–17	252
13:24–35	214
13:34–35	59, 84, 87, 123, 173, 202, 215
14	152
14:1–4	190
14:1–6	202
14:6	81
14:27	142, 156
15:12–13	202
15:15	87
16:1–4	248
17:17	81
20:24–31	157
21:20	181

Acts

1:1	26, 250
1:14	173
2	238
2:22–23	82
2:36–39	82
2:41–47	173
2:42–47	33, 202
2:44–46	232
2:44–47	1
2:46–47	182
2:47	33, 205
4:13	50
4:32	173
4:32–5:11	232
5	234
5:41	31, 252
6:1–7	173
7	86
7:54–60	126
7:60	135
9:4	76
9:23–25	239
9:26–30	239
9:36–43	190
10:2	196
11	191
11:20–24	235
13:2	33
13:45	86
14:1–7	86
16	242
16:1–3	227

16:6–7	192	12:10–16	205
16:29	149	12:11–21	192
17:5–9	86	12:14–21	176
17:22–29	27	12:15	2, 77, 80, 157
17:28	166, 240		
17:30–31	197	12:15–21	216
18:26	6, 239	12:16–21	229
20:26–27	213	12:17–21	30, 224
20:27	220	12:18	156, 228–229
20:35	203	12:18–21	90
20:36–38	173	12:21	223
21:26–36	86	14	107
22:1–21	191	16:1–2	190
22:22–24	86	16:24	182
23:1–5	216	**1 Corinthians**	
23:12ff	239	1:4–9	196
26:24–29	112	1:10	173
Romans		2:3	149
1:8–12	196	3:1–3	254
1:8–13	173, 202	4:1–5	25, 226
1:8–15	192	4:17	32–33
1:16	103	5:7	33
1:17	204	6:7	227
1:18–32	218	9:19–23	215
3:9–18	218	10:12	23, 78, 101, 237
3:23	23, 245		
3:23–24	42	10:13	105
5:1–11	236	11:1	58, 197, 219
5:5–8	59	12	3, 227, 242
5:6–8	21	12:4–31	102–103
5:6–11	190	12:26–27	173
6:3	204	13	87, 183, 202, 253
8	236		
8:26	63	13:4–7	79
8:31–39	192, 229, 248	13:5	28
12:1–2	190	13:7	77
12:3	23, 78, 100, 102, 233–234, 245	13:7–8a	71
		13:8	207
12:3–13	190	15:33	127, 179, 218
12:3–21	248	15:58	10, 204, 229
12:4–13	3, 102	16:13–18	182
12:9	77	16:15	196
12:9–13	173	16:15–16	7, 58
12:9–21	1		

2 Corinthians

1:3–4	165, 216
4–5	152
4:7	204
4:7–16	248
4:7–18	254
4:16–5:7	217
4:16–5:11	32, 233
5:9–11	56, 107
5:10–11	204
5:12–21	202
5:13	112
5:13–21	21
7:2–12	52
7:5	149
7:8–9	253
7:8–12	153
7:10	216, 246, 253–254
8	238
8:1–5	202
8:1–7	232
8:12	238
9:6	203
10:15	157
11:23ff	80
11:28–29	80, 196
12	54, 216
12:7–10	158, 208
12:28–29	217
13:5	24, 205, 234

Galatians

2:1–10	228
2:11	228
2:11–18	148
2:11–21	219
2:13	250
2:14	228
4:16	213
5:19–21	126, 233
5:20	28
5:22–23	38, 228
5:22–25	182
5:22–26	183, 263
6:1	3
6:1–2	4, 23
6:1–5	107, 156
6:1–10	103
6:2	2, 22, 79–80, 217
6:3	102
6:5	217
6:6–10	59
6:9	189
6:9–10	141, 202, 216
6:10	22, 27, 176

Ephesians

1:15–23	196
2:10	22
2:19–22	173
4	126
4:11	197
4:11–15	93
4:11–16	3, 56–57, 102, 183, 240, 242, 251
4:12	240
4:13	58, 200
4:15	52, 215
4:17–32	1
4:25	197, 213
4:26	253
4:26–27	126
4:28	198
4:29	51, 241
4:29–32	214, 222
4:29–33	134
4:31	126
4:32	77, 173
5:25–30	236
5:28	27
6:1–3	223
6:4	221, 251
6:5–8	197
6:12	17
6:18	201

Philippians

1–4	252
1:3–7	196

1:12–14	152	**2 Thessalonians**	
1:15–18	97	1:3	157
2:1–3	237	2:10	81
2:1–4	59, 123, 173, 227	3:11–12	212
		1 Timothy	
2:3	233	2:1–6	201
2:3–4	4, 27, 64, 83, 96, 157, 202, 215	2:3–5	21
		2:3–6	21
2:4	2, 22, 77, 236	2:4	81, 240
		3:1–2	233
2:5–11	203, 232	3:1–7	7
2:12–13	202, 204	4:11–5:2	3
2:13	240	4:12–16	175, 196, 204, 219
2:20–21	232		
2:25–30	182	6:3–5	196
3:17	58, 197, 219	6:6–7	32
4:1–3	156	6:18–19	32
4:4	96, 141, 252	**2 Timothy**	
4:4–9	55, 241	1:3–5	175
4:6	202	1:3–7	205
4:8–9	141	1:7	49, 147, 156
4:9	219	2:1–7	2
4:10–19	182	3:1–5	28, 218
4:11	140	3:2	231
4:11–13	97	3:5	234
4:13	100, 208	3:10–17	5
4:18	190	3:14–17	57
4:18a	97	3:16–17	37, 247
Colossians		4:3	211
1:3–8	196	4:3–4	153, 219
3:6	215	4:4	212
3:12–17	56, 173, 241	4:9–16	172
3:14	77	**Titus**	
3:22–24	197	1:12	196
3:23	10	1:16	26, 196
3:23–24	71	2:1	3
4:6	169, 222	2:1–8	2, 175
1 Thessalonians		2:3–5	3
1:2–4	196	2:6–8	175
4:9–10	10, 71, 79, 173	2:7	22, 196
		2:10	27
5:14	55, 216	2:14	22, 196, 202, 204
5:17	168, 193		
5:18	201–202	2:24–26	228

3:1	196	2:11–12	190, 202, 248
3:1–7	216	2:17	173
3:8	22, 196	2:18–25	31
3:9–11	196, 229	2:23	253
3:14	22, 196	3:1–12	223
Philemon		3:8–18	229
7	190	3:14	228
Hebrews		3:15–16	229
4:15	75	3:17	84
6:4–8	238	4:8	39
10:14	252	4:8–10	173
10:24	202, 205	4:10	71, 141
10:24–25	141	4:12–14	252
10:25		4:16	228
10:32–34	228	5:5–7	102, 237
10:34	31	5:6	57
11:1	204	5:6–7	165
11:4	246	5:7	157
11:6	103, 204	5:8	15
12:1–2	203	**2 Peter**	
12:2	96, 252	1	79, 263
13:1–3	173	1:1	205
13:7	7, 147, 156	1:5–8	56
13:17	7, 107	1:5–11	157, 182–183
James		1:8–11	204
1:5	168, 205, 214	1:12–13	248
1:13	75	3:10–12	32
1:16	126	**1 John**	
1:17	51	1:6	26
1:19	61, 196, 203	2:15–16	32
1:19–20	3, 127	3:11	77
1:22–25	24	3:14	77
2:14–26	201	3:16–18	202
3:13–18	229	3:17	27
3:14	233	3:18	248
3:16	233	3:19–20	243
4:4	32, 179	3–4	173
4:6	235	4:7–8	77
5:16	54	4:7–11	64
5:19–20	19	4:7–5:6	241
1 Peter		4:8	63
1:13–16	22, 126	4:9–11	22
1:22	84	4:11	2
2:5	190	4:18	147

4:19–21	202
4:21	39
5:3	241

2 John

7–8	7

3 John

9	235

Jude

3	229
3–10	219
9	229
22–23	19

Revelation

1:17	147
2:7	61
2:8–9	246
2:8–11	202
2:11	61
2:17	61
2:20–23	219
2:29	61
3:6	61
3:13	61
3:14–22	235
3:16	185
3:22	61
21:1–27	202
21:4	217
21:8	147, 213

ABOUT THE AUTHORS

Bill Bagents earned his master's degree in counselor education from Auburn University and doctor of ministry from Amridge University. He is currently professor of ministry, counseling, and biblical studies with Heritage Christian University. He has served as an elder, deacon, and minister as well as working as a counselor with the Alpha Center. His wife, Laura, teaches with Florence City Schools. Bill has taught counseling courses in Bangladesh, Nigeria, the Philippines, and South Africa.

Rosemary Snodgrass, licensed professional counselor, earned her doctorate in counselor education from the University of Alabama. She transitioned from a successful career as a school counselor to teaching both graduate and undergraduate courses for Heritage Christian University. Before retiring, she served as director of the Alpha Center, a Christian counseling center, in Florence, Alabama. Her husband, Don, is an elder with the Sherrod Avenue Church of Christ. Rosemary has taught counseling courses in the Philippines and South Africa.

ALSO BY HERITAGE CHRISTIAN
UNIVERSITY PRESS IN COOPERATION
WITH HERITAGE CHRISTIAN
LEADERSHIP INSTITUTE

Lead Like the Lord: Lessons in Leadership from Jesus

by W. Kirk Brothers (2021)

Corrupt Communication: Myths that Target Church Leaders

by Bill Bagents and Laura S. Bagents (Forthcoming)

www.ingramcontent.com/pod-product-compliance
Lightning Source LLC
Chambersburg PA
CBHW071805080526
44589CB00012B/692